Chapter One

What Causes Stress

In today's world, it is difficult to avoid experiencing feelings of exhaustion from time to time. When you have to balance the demands of job, family, and other responsibilities, it's easy to feel overwhelmed and stressed out. But you really must schedule some time in your schedule to relax, or else both your mental and physical health might suffer.

Practice Takes Time

It will take some time and effort on your part to master the art of stress management, but you can and should make the effort.

Regular physical activity is one of the most effective methods to relax both the body and the mind. In addition, regular exercise will improve your mood. However, in order for it to be beneficial, you will need to perform it often.

A good technique to use is exercising for up to two at a moderate intensity, such as brisk walking, or exercise for up to one hour at a more strenuous intensity, such as running, swimming laps, or other sports.

Concentrate on accomplishing the fitness objectives you set for yourself so that you don't give up. Remember, above all else, that getting any kind of physical activity is preferable to getting none at all.

Relax Your Mind And Body

If your muscles stiffen up under pressure. By yourself, you may help loosen them up and revitalize your body by:

- ☐ Stretching
- ☐ Having a relaxing massage
- ☐ Getting in a steamy shower or bath
- ☐ Having a restful sleep

Just Breathe

Taking a moment to pause and breathe deeply may alleviate stress almost instantly. Once you master it, you'll be astonished at the difference it makes in your wellbeing. Here are the 5 simple steps:

- ☐ **<u>Step One:</u>** Put your feet up and get into a relaxed sitting posture. You may also lay down.
- ☐ **<u>Step Two</u>**: Put your eyes close.
- ☐ **<u>Step Three</u>**: Try to picture yourself in a tranquil setting. It doesn't have to be a specific place; wherever that makes you feel at ease would do.
- ☐ **<u>Step Four</u>**: Take a few deep breaths and relax.
- ☐ **<u>Step Five</u>**: Take breaks of 5 to 10 minutes to do this.

Eat Good To Feel Good

Feeling healthier overall might be attributed to sticking to a healthy eating routine. The regulation of your emotions may also benefit. Vegetables, fruits, healthy grains, and lean protein will provide you with the most energy from the food you eat. And be sure to complete them in order. It's terrible for you, may make you cranky, and adds stress to your life.

Slow Down. Stop, And Smell The Roses

Life in the modern world is so busy, and sometimes all we need to do is slow down and relax. Look at your life and figure out how you can do that in small ways. For instance:

Because the modern world is so hectic, it's important to remember to take it easy every once in a while and simply relax. Take a look at your life and see if there are any little ways that you can do that. Take, for instance:

Adjust your watch by five to ten minutes ahead of time. That way, you'll arrive at your destinations a little bit early and save yourself the anxiety of running late.

If you want to avoid becoming angry on the road, it's best to drive in the slow lane while you're on the highway.

Convert large tasks into a series of smaller ones. For instance, if you aren't required to respond to all 100 emails, don't bother trying to do so; instead, focus on responding to a select handful of them.

What's In Your Schedule

You need to make time in your schedule for some genuine relaxation in order to give your mind a break from the strain of the situation. If you are the kind of person who enjoys establishing objectives for themselves, you may find this to be challenging at first. But if you keep going, you'll get to the point where you look forward to these situations. Activities such as the following may help you relax:

- ☐ Meditation
- ☐ Yoga
- ☐ Prayer
- ☐ Enjoying some of your favorite music as you relax.
- ☐ Time spent in the great outdoors

Do What You Love To Do

You must schedule time for your favorite activities. Doing something enjoyable can help you feel better and reduce stress. Try to do this every day. Even 15 to one hour will suffice; it doesn't need to be a long period of time. Among the activities that are relaxing are: reading, knitting, creating a work of art, taking up golf, viewing a film. solve puzzle, board games and card games.

Conversate To Elevate

If you're feeling stressed, having a conversation about what's upsetting you might help. You may speak to those closest to you, such family and friends, as well as professionals like your doctor and therapist.

Time To Have A Talk With You

You can have a conversation with yourself, too. We all engage in this practice, known as self-talk. For self-talk to be effective in the reduction of stress, however, it must be positive rather than negative.

When you're feeling anxious, pay careful attention to what you're saying and thinking. If you're telling yourself anything bad, try telling yourself something good instead. Avoid negative self-talk by avoiding statements like "I cant." Remind yourself positive affirmations like "I think I can. I think I can. I think I can." or "I'm doing the best I can."

What's The Cause Here?

Find out what is causing you the most stress. Is it your work, your travel time, or your studies? If you know what they are, you can work to get rid of or at least significantly lessen their impact on your life.

Keeping a stress diary will help you figure out what's causing your anxiety if nothing else. Keep track of your nervous moments to see if you can identify a trend and then work to mitigate its effects.

Chapter Two

A Little Change Helps You Grow

In today's modern world, the concepts of stress and change are often confused with one another. A change in a circumstance that both the body and the mind feel to be overpowering might trigger the physiological and psychological reaction known as stress.

At times, life may seem overwhelming and stressful because of the quick speed at which it moves both at work and at home, the continual barrage of technological distractions, and the need to still find time to interact with people who are close by. You could ask this question to yourself very frequently: "How should I manage my stress?"

Meditate To Elevate

A fantastic method to divert your attention away from the strains of day-to-day living is to participate in guided meditation. There are several guided meditations accessible online that will assist you in finding five minutes of calm relaxation. You can access these meditations via the internet.

The Nervous System

The activation of a person's sympathetic nervous system, which regulates the body's reaction of "fight or flight" to a perceived danger, may be reduced by practicing deep breathing, which is an excellent method. Inhaling deeply for a count of five seconds, holding your breath for two seconds, then exhaling for a count of five seconds may assist activate your parasympathetic nervous system, allowing it to relax and digest. This, in turn, helps lower the overall tension and anxiety that you may be feeling.

By slowing your breathing, you may calm your sympathetic nervous system, which regulates your body's "fight or flight" reaction to danger. By stimulating the parasympathetic nerve system, which is responsible for relaxation and digestion, deep breaths in for a count of five seconds, held for a count of two seconds, then released for a count of five seconds may help alleviate tension and anxiety.

Maybe A Diet Could Be More Helpful?

The way you react to stress is significantly influenced by a number of factors, including diet and physical activity. It is possible for your mind to be healthy when your body is healthy, and vice versa. Exercising has been shown to be an effective method of relieving stress and also contributes to an improvement in one's overall quality of life.. Not only does maintaining healthy eating help your body feel better, but it also helps your mind feel better, which enables you to better resist the negative effects of stress.

How you handle stress depends on several factors, including your diet and regular exercise. A sound physical condition may facilitate a sound mental state, and vice versa. Exercising regularly has been shown to reduce stress and increase happiness levels. Keeping up a healthy diet not only benefits the body, but also the mind, making it easier to deal with stress.

Time Better Spent

It's not only the content of social networking sites that may be stressful; the time spent there might be better spent relaxing with friends, basking in the sun, or reading a good book. Many individuals also use social media late at night, which may be stressful just when they're trying to wind down for the night, leading to less hours of quality sleep overall.

Love Feels Good

Humans thrive in group settings. To feel loved and cared for, you need to develop relationships with other people. It's beneficial to your health to participate in activities that bring you together with others, such as team sports or church groups. Sharing in a common interest is a great way to make friends and build ties that may help you through tough times.

An Unusual Amount Of Stressful Situations

If you're feeling an unacceptable amount of mental stress, it's important to take steps to reduce the sources of that stress. The way you internalize a stressful situation also has a significant role in how you react to it. Stressful situations and problems are not always avoidable, but you may take steps to lessen their impact. Consider if you can make a change in the stressful situation, such as letting go of certain responsibilities, lowering your expectations, or reaching out for assistance.

Have A Support System

Increase your stress resistance by building a strong social support system. Strategically make contact. Some loved ones and companions may have excellent listening and empathetic skills. Some people are more adept than others in providing concrete assistance, such as preparing and delivering a meal or watching the kids for an hour. The act of helping another person might have a similarly elevating effect on their mood. Maintain harmony in your connections at all costs. A buddy who always needs help but never provides it might be adding to your burden.

Watch What You Eat

Seek for nutritious foods; the release of adrenaline and cortisol from the central nervous system in response to stress has physiological effects, including on the digestive system. The production of the hormone cortisol during chronic stress may promote fat and sugar cravings, in contrast to the suppressed appetite seen during acute stress. Visceral fat, which is linked to cardiovascular and metabolic illnesses, may be deposited around our internal organs when stress levels are high and sugar intake is high, according to studies. Protecting health and boosting energy levels to take on difficulties head-on are two benefits of eating a diet rich in a wide range of nutrients. There's no need to give up cookies in favor of eating a rainbow's worth of fruits and veggies every day. Substances like alcohol should be avoided to reduce the stress response since they do not address the underlying cause of the issue and may have detrimental health implications.

Take Good Care Of Your Body

Take care of your body by eating well and relaxing your muscles when you feel stressed. Tension in the muscles results from stress, which may lead to pain in the head, back, and elsewhere, as well as overall exhaustion. Stretching, massage, and hot showers may all help alleviate stress and its associated symptoms. You might also try progressive muscle relaxation, a technique that has been demonstrated to help with both anxiety and general well-being. First, choose a comfortable posture, and then select a muscle group, such as your lower leg muscles (most professionals advise beginning with the lower body and working your way up). For five to ten seconds while inhaling, tense your muscles; then, while exhaling, release the tension all at once. After working a certain muscle group, let it rest for at least 10 seconds before moving on. P.M.R., or passive progressive muscle relaxation, is still another choice. This method is quite similar to progressive muscle relaxation, however it does not begin with tensing the muscles first. Instead, visualize individual muscle groups and bring your attention to relaxing those areas.

Mindfulness

Mindful meditation has been shown to alleviate psychological stress and anxiety, and even brief mindfulness meditation courses have shown positive results. First, choose a peaceful spot to sit for five minutes and just breathe. Pay attention in the here and now; if distracting ideas arise, label them as such and let them go. If you find your thoughts fluctuating, give yourself a break. Calmly return one's thoughts back to the here and now. Relaxation. This method is quite similar to progressive muscle relaxation, however it does not begin with tensing the muscles first. Instead, visualize individual muscle groups and bring your attention to relaxing those areas.

Getting Through The Days

The stress of the day might disrupt your rest at night. Lack of sleep worsens the problem since it alters both mood and cognitive performance. Better sleep techniques. Maintain a regular bedtime routine that enables you to unwind before you go to sleep. Sleeplessness may be alleviated by the practice of meditation and relaxation. In addition, stay away from the coffee and alcohol as the evening approaches. Blue light from screens may prevent the production of melatonin, which helps you go asleep, and browsing social media might make you feel more emotional, so put them down. Lastly, remember to keep moving throughout the day: There is a substantial body of evidence indicating that exercise, particularly among middle-aged and older persons, may enhance sleep quality.

Chapter Three

One Step Forward

Get moving: brisk walking has been shown to reduce stress and enhance sleep quality. Moderate exercisers had 50% less stress at work than their inactive counterparts, according to one research. Stress may negatively affect the immune system, but doing moderate exercise may help mitigate this effect. Including exercise doesn't have to add a lot of hassle or cost: A vigorous 30-minute stroll or an in-house dance party can do the job.

Physical activity reduces stress and improves sleep. among one research, moderate physical exercise reduced stress among working people by half. Stress may also weaken the immune system, although exercise may mitigate this. It's easy to add exercise: A little 30-minute stroll or living room dancing might help.

Find Pleasure

Keep your entertaining. If life becomes hectic, individuals frequently forsake their hobbies first. But denying oneself pleasure might backfire. Find time to read a book, sing your favorite songs, or watch a Netflix comedy series, even if time is limited. Laughter improves mental and physical wellbeing.

Cognitive Therapy

CBT is a proven stress and anxiety treatment. This therapeutic method recognizes that ideas affect emotions and behavior. Rethinking a stressor may reduce stress. Some advice: Stop thinking worst-case scenarios and focus on anything else. Expect realistically. Accept uncontrollable events.

Reframe your thinking. Cognitive behavioral therapy, sometimes known as CBT, is one of the therapies for stress and anxiety that has received the greatest support from studies. This kind of psychotherapy is predicated on the realization that our ideas have an effect on our feelings, which, in turn, have an effect on the actions we engage in. It is possible to better control your emotions and, as a result, experience less stress by changing the way you think about the things that are stressful to you. A few pointers: If you find yourself beginning to imagine the worst possible outcomes, you should immediately stop and redirect your thoughts to something else. Establish reasonable goals and standards for yourself. Make an effort to accept the things that are happening that you can't change.

Get Help

Seek assistance: If you are feeling overwhelmed and you are not finding that self-help is working, search for a psychologist or another mental health specialist who can teach you how to successfully manage your stress and assist you in learning how to handle it efficiently. They will be able to assist you in determining the circumstances or actions that are contributing to your stress, after which they will assist you in developing a strategy to alter the stressors, modify your surroundings, and change your reactions.

The feeling of stress may be either acute or chronic, depending on how long it lasts. Acute stress is often a reaction to a stressor that only lasts for a brief period of time, such as being in a vehicle accident or having a fight with your partner. Acute stress may be quite upsetting, but it normally passes fast and responds well to coping tactics such as slowing one's breathing or engaging in vigorous physical exercise.

What Causes Stress?

Continuous exposure to stimuli is what causes chronic stress. Chronic stress may have a broad variety of causes, ranging from circumstances that individuals can manage or steer clear of (like having a toxic relationship) to challenges that are tough to circumvent. Since individuals react differently to stressful situations, a scenario that one person would find bearable might become a source of ongoing stress for another person. This is because people respond differently to stressful situations.

Long-term stress may be harmful to one's physical as well as mental health. If you are always under pressure, you may find that it makes you feel tired, reduces your capacity to focus, gives you headaches, and makes it harder to digest food. People who are predisposed to irritable bowel syndrome often discover that their symptoms worsen when they are under emotional stress. Even while short-term or acute stress may boost certain immune responses, long-term or chronic stress is harmful to the immune system because it causes wear and tear on the system. Multiple studies have shown a correlation between chronic stress and the development of coronary artery disease. This suggests that chronic stress may potentially have an effect on the health of the heart.

What Is Stress Exactly?

The reaction of your body to an adversity or a demand is called stress. Everyone has gone through stressful times, which may have been brought on by a wide variety of circumstances, ranging from little annoyances that occur on a daily basis to life-altering catastrophes such as being divorced or losing a job. The physical components of the stress reaction include things like an increased heart rate and blood pressure. Mental components include things like ideas and personal views about the stressful experience. Emotional components include things like dread and rage.

Although we often think of it as being negative, stress can also come from positive changes in your life, like getting a promotion at work or having a new baby,"

Challenges or demands cause stress. Everybody has gotten stressed, from little annoyances to severe life crises like divorce or job loss. Stress reaction involves physical symptoms like raised heart rate and blood pressure, thoughts and ideas about the stressful experience, and emotions like fear and wrath.

Some individuals drink or overeat to relieve stress. These activities may appear helpful, but they may actually increase stress. Caffeine increases stress. Eating well reduces stress.

These acts could seem to be helpful in the now, but in the long term, they might really contribute more stress to your life. Additionally, caffeine might amplify the negative consequences of stress. Consuming a diet that is both nutritious and well-balanced is one way to assist in the fight against stress.

Smoking Is Not Good For You

Many people who use nicotine refer to it as a stress reliever while they are doing so. On the other hand, nicotine causes your body more stress through elevating your level of physical arousal and slowing both the circulatory system and your respiration. In addition, it is possible for it to aggravate chronic pain; thus, if you are suffering persistent stress and bodily pains, smoking will not be of any use to you.

Managing Stress

Managing stress and protecting your body from the negative consequences of stress are both made easier when you make the effort to relax on a daily basis. You have access to a wide range of strategies, such as slow and deep breathing, guided imagery, progressive muscle relaxation, and mindfulness meditation, amongst others. There are a lot of websites and applications for smartphones that provide instruction on these methods. Although there are some that have a fee associated with them, there are as plenty that are completely free.

To Do's

It's possible that your life has too many demands for the amount of time you have available, especially if you're like most people. The majority of these requirements are ones that we have decided to implement. However, you may make more time for yourself by developing skills in time management, such as asking for assistance when it is warranted, establishing priorities, pacing yourself, and setting aside time to care for you.

Chapter Four

The Human Experience

Each of us has gone through periods of both physical and emotional agony. Being annoyed because of the pain is very normal. The distinction is that some people hold on to those painful memories longer than others, making it more difficult for them to move on with their life. It's normal to become stuck and replay your experience, but you must eventually learn to put the past and future out of your mind and concentrate on the here and now. It's time to master the art of letting go.

If you continue to feel that agony, you can end up doing more harm to yourself. It's crucial to acquire coping mechanisms so that you can get past that particular experience and begin to heal yourself.

Some individuals hang onto such terrible events and struggle to move on. It's easy to become trapped and rehash your experience, but you need to concentrate on the present. Learn to let go.

Holding onto that pain might injure you more. It's important to learn how to cope with that suffering, put that scenario behind you, and recover by retaining just what will help you develop and go on.

Don't Suppress Emotions

Don't suppress grief and frustration. Let yourself experience unpleasant emotions like happy ones. It's okay to feel unhappy and grieve, but it's unhealthy to allow those sentiments take control and create new emotions.

Express your hurts anyway you wish. Speak up. Talk to your pals, write down your ideas, express them out loud even if nobody is listening, yell, weep, and do whatever you need to relieve the agony. This can help you understand how you actually feel and why the circumstance affects you so you can accept and move on.

Do not suppress your feelings of pain and frustration when you find yourself in a situation where you have to cope with them. Give yourself permission to experience your less desirable feelings in the same manner that you do your more desirable ones. It is natural for people to have feelings of sadness on occasion and to go through the stages of the grieving process. However, it is not good to allow these sentiments to take control of you and to give rise to new sensations.

Give vent to your emotions and find a method to verbalize the things that cause you pain in whatever manner is most comfortable for you. Find your voice and let others listen to what you have to say. Scream your head off, weep your eyes out, talk it out with your pals, write down your ideas, utter them out loud even if nobody is there to hear you, do whatever it takes to get the anguish out of your system and liberate yourself. You will have a better understanding of how you really feel about the situation and the reasons why it hurts you as a result of doing this, which will enable you to accept it and put it in the past.

Time To Let Go

To get rid of those unpleasant feelings for good, you must first decide to change. Letting go takes intentional effort. Commit to your choice. Stop rehashing previous events. Even though it's challenging at first, you'll notice how far you've gone since making this decision.

Willpower matters. Distract yourself and recall your commitment when you want to rehash a problem or resent something. Adopt a healthy lifestyle and learn from terrible experiences.

If you feel as if those bad feelings are taking up too much room in your heart and head, the first step you need to do to rid yourself of them once and for all is to make the deliberate decision that you want to make some kind of adjustment in your life. It takes a deliberate effort and a conscious choice to acquire the skill of letting go of things. You need to make a commitment, both to yourself and to the choice you've made. From that point forward, make an effort to avoid revisiting previous situations. Even though it is challenging at first, in due time you will be able to look back and realize how far you have gone as a result of making this decision.

The use of one's willpower is really necessary here. Distract your thoughts and bring to mind the promise you made whenever you have the need to dwell on the specifics of a problem or to feel frustrated about the things that have caused you pain. Accept a new healthy way of life and direct your attention to the lessons that may be drawn from those difficult experiences.

Pause On The Replay

It's typical to replay sad memories and details. Wishing for alternative moments can keep you from living fully. Unfortunately, you cannot alter the past. Stop reliving a moment that will never change.

Retelling a painful tale is pointless. Reliving that pain will hurt you more. Instead of repeating the tale, accept the circumstance and plan for the future. Imagine yourself in a similar circumstance. You'll know how to manage things so you don't hurt again.

It is not uncommon to realize that you are reliving traumatic experiences and going over every detail that causes you to feel anguish again and again. The only thing that will keep you from enjoying a life to the fullest is wishing that these times were different. Unfortuitously, no one can reverse the past, and there is nothing that can be done to alter the results of things that have already happened. Recognize the truth and refrain from dwelling on the past since it is impossible to change the past.

There is no use in continuing to tell a tale that has the same conclusion, which is suffering. You will just end up hurting yourself worse if you allow yourself to go through this painful experience again. Instead of continually rehashing the same narrative in your head, you should realize the reality of the issue and make plans on how to go going forward. Let's say you end yourself in a circumstance that's quite similar to this one. You will have a better understanding of how to deal with difficult situations, which will prevent you from experiencing pain in the future.

Don't Place Blame On Others

On a negative viewpoint that is not healthy, blaming others makes unpleasant circumstances easier. You might believe someone wronged you and the other person may think the same. Victimizing yourself and blaming someone else might feel fantastic.

It's appropriate to seek an apology, make them realize what they did. Blaming others for your misery gives them influence over your emotions. This hinders letting go.

As previously said, you must accept that things are as they are and that blaming others will not alter them. Stop blaming others, accept responsibility, and move on.

You may continue to believe that someone has wronged you, and the other person may continue to believe the same thing about you. It is possible that it will make you feel better to play the victim role, absolve yourself of responsibility, and place the blame on another person who may or may not be to blame.

In circumstances such as these, it is appropriate to want an apology, to demand that they admit what they did.If you blame another person for your suffering, you are, in effect, giving that person the ability to dictate how you feel about what happened. This will just prevent you from letting go of the situation.

You need to accept that things are the way they are and that blaming other people will not affect the outcome of what has transpired. I have told this to you previously. Therefore, stop pointing the finger at other people, acknowledge your part in the predicament, and move on from it.

Chapter Five

Surround Yourself With Good Company

Surround yourself with people who love and want the best for you. Remember that relatives and close associates will always support you.

Talk to your supporters about how you feel. Realizing you're safe, release every unpleasant emotion. Listen to their outsider viewpoint to get a new perspective. Even if their views differ from yours, consider them.

Take a break from negative individuals if you live with them. Creating distance from unimportant individuals might help you let go.

Find comfort in the people who satisfy you, speak to them about how you feel, and discuss what you're going through with them. You are now in a safe and supportive atmosphere; thus, it is important that you work through all of the terrible emotions that you are experiencing. Listen to what they have to say since they will provide you with an objective viewpoint that will assist you in gaining a new understanding of the circumstance. Even if you disagree with them, try to have a cheerful attitude and an open mind while considering their points of view.

If you find yourself living with people that do not make a good contribution to your life, the best thing you can do is create some space between yourself and these individuals. There are instances when putting distance between yourself and individuals who aren't required may be a significant step toward letting go.

Purpose

For the purpose of trying to let go easier, concentrate on the now and make the most of it. Continue your day with pleasant ideas and enjoyable activities. When the anguish overwhelms you, do what makes you happy.

in order to make this process easier on yourself, you should concentrate on the here and now and do all you can to make the most of it. Carry on with your day by thinking optimistic thoughts and engaging in things that make you feel good about yourself. Distract yourself with the things that bring you pleasure in the here and now whenever you have the feeling that the suffering is about to take control.

Leaving the past in the past and concentrating on the here and now will allow room for new experiences to enter your life. This will clear your mind of all the bad feelings and allow you to create place in it for new concepts that will contribute to your progress. As you make room in your life for pleasure and happiness, you will quickly come to the conclusion that releasing your grip on the situation was the finest decision you could have made.

Focusing upon the present frees up room for fresh viewpoints. This will clear your head of negative emotions and create place for growth-oriented thinking. As you embrace love and happiness, you'll realize letting go was the finest decision.

Quit a miserable job. Drop negative memories.

Let It Go

There are other ways to let go of the things that harm you. Professionals assist individuals recover from trauma. Therapists are often forbidden. However, consulting a professional is not shameful. Many individuals should speak to a stranger instead of a friend or themselves.

Going to an expert may help you overcome a difficult event and teach you important life lessons. It may even assist with a problem you didn't realize you had.

there are specialists that assist individuals in overcoming the effects of traumatic situations. There is a widespread stigma attached to seeking help from a mental health professional. Nevertheless, there is no shame in seeking the assistance of a trained expert, and there is no need to feel guilty about doing so. Instead of going to a friend or attempting to figure things out on their own, many individuals might benefit by having a conversation with a stranger who does not know them.

Going to a professional can not only help you move on from a negative experience and guide you through the process of overcoming it, but it will also provide you with a great deal of useful information that you can incorporate into your day-to-day life. These are just two of the many advantages that can be gained by consulting with an expert. It may even assist you with something that you didn't even realize was a struggle for you.

A guided meditation for letting go will help you let go of traumatic events between professional sessions.

In the time that you are not working with a mental health professional, you may find it helpful to practice letting go of traumatic events with the assistance of a guided meditation.

Getting Over It, To Peace

Getting over old relationships, events, and memories is hard. Do not tend to dwell on bad ideas and events. Even though this reasoning helps us avoid danger and react fast, it was not meant to dwell on constantly. You have to move on and live your life. This method of thinking enables us to stay out of harm's way and act swiftly during times of crisis, which is important from an evolutionary point of view. However, after the risk has been eliminated, what steps should we take next? How can we proceed when the threat has passed?

Some individuals can't let go of terrible memories or relationships because they think their past defines them. Some individuals have a difficult time letting go of bad memories or relationships, or moving on from the effects of previous events, because they think that whatever has occurred to them is an essential component of who they are.

However, dwelling on the past and clinging to grief won't help. Dwelling on the past won't make it go away, and refusing to let go of painful memories won't make it easier to move on from them.

Establish Expectations

Establish expectations for how long you want to endure the sorrow, loss, or discomfort before accepting and moving on. You should prepare yourself with some expectations for the amount of time you will spend feeling the sorrow, loss, or discomfort before you are able to graduate to acceptance and go on.

How can I know how much time I need before I start processing? How long do you need? An hour of digesting a negative memory may help you forget it. After a breakup, you may need a month to recover, think, and be with yourself before moving on. If you loss a loved one, you may want to be comforted by the next holiday you would have spent with or on their anniversary. How long you dwell with old trauma might vary.

If you are troubled by a negative memory that you would want to put behind you, spending one hour properly digesting it can be all that is required to help you do so. If you are currently dealing with the aftermath of a breakup, you should probably give yourself at least a month to relax, think, and spend time with yourself before deciding whether or not you have successfully moved on.

How long you want to stay with these sensations may also reveal how important something is to you. Maybe you'll discover that something was bearing more weight on your mind or heart than you wanted to afford, or that something or someone was much more significant to you than you imagined, and you'll need more time to process and better methods to deal.

You decide the timeline. You won't know what's right for you unless you think about it!

Chapter Six

Processing

Whether you choose to process on your own through journaling or if you decide to use a voice recorder and speak to yourself out loud, you can do so by hand or by computer, phone or device that allows you to write on it.

As part of this, you might want to journal, talk to someone close to you, or work with a therapist or coach so that you can express yourself.

Whether you choose to process on your own through journaling or if you decide to use a voice recorder and speak to yourself out loud, you can do so by hand or by computer, phone or device that allows you to write on it.

Studies have shown that those who journal about key experiences report higher pleasure with their life and better mental health than those who did not, but whichever manner works best for you is the appropriate way.

It is important to take a moment to digest and reflect before releasing and progressing forward.

Effectively expressing the sequence of events, the knowledge gained, personal growth achieved, and the aspects to relinquish, along with visualizing the outcome of your release, will furnish you with the necessary resources to execute your plan of letting go.

Dealing with things or individuals that you wish to leave behind can be challenging. It necessitates bravery to confront recollections, feelings, and thoughts that might be upsetting or problematic. However, by enduring the discomfort and dedicating time to comprehend and construct a solid action plan, you can find the most comforting way to release them and move on. If additional support is required, connect with a counselor who will offer assistance throughout the entire process.

<u>Journaling Prompts To Consider:</u>

- ☐ Why do you want to move on from what happened? What do you want to be free of? Did something happen that you want to let go of? Take some time to brainstorm and jot down or speak freely about the specific event, person, or memory that you wish to move past. Express all your thoughts either in written form or through communication. If it feels appropriate, you have the option to complete it in multiple sessions. Observe your emotions prior to and after you release all your thoughts onto a document or through verbal communication. Afterward, go through what you've written, pay attention to what you've spoken, or inquire with the person you're conversing with to understand their interpretation of your words. Begin observing if any recurring patterns become evident, or if supplementary emotions arise and document them accordingly.

☐ What lessons and transformations have you experienced as a result of the thing or person you desire to release? It's understandable if you are unaware of the solution, and that is perfectly fine. Allow your thoughts to guide you. What was the state of things prior to the occurrence or partnership you wish to leave behind, and how do they compare to the present? If a considerable duration has elapsed, have you observed any transformations within yourself since the incident in question, and how do you respond to these alterations? What remains of the influence of this circumstance or individual on you? While you may have the desire to progress, it is not mandatory to forsake all that you have at present. Consider whether there are any possessions or items that you wish to keep or bring along with you. This encompasses acquired knowledge and personal qualities that have developed and strengthened over time.

☐ What are the specific things that you wish to release
or relinquish?
Naming the things you desire to release can
significantly aid in your cognitive processing. Do they
refer to your sentiments, views or distinct perceptions
regarding a circumstance or individual, your actions or
impact on others, or the modifications or progression
of your surroundings?

☐ Would there be a particular appearance or sensation
associated with releasing this entity or individual? Use
your imagination to picture how things will appear,
make you feel or sound after you have moved on.
How do you envision your presentation? What
qualities would your relationships posses? How would
you describe your work and personal life? As this is
an exercise in visualization, delve deep into the
details of your desired outcomes. Any format that
suits your needs is acceptable, be it a story, a list, a
cluster of words, or even images. A smart paraphrase
of this text could be: By speaking to yourself, another
person, or by recording your thoughts, you can
articulate your vision of an ideal day after leaving a
particular situation, or the emotional state you
anticipate upon letting go of someone or something.
As your visualization gradually develops, you'll begin
to sense that you can truly embody this
transformation. Devise a well thought-out strategy
outlining the necessary steps required to initiate

progress. Initially, identify the disparities between your mental image and current situation, and contemplate on the measures that can be implemented to connect the two. What steps can you take to transition from your current situation to where you would be if you moved forward? Are there minor actions you could initiate to begin the process of releasing your attachment? What activities do you plan on engaging in, whether it be today, this week, this month, or this year, in order to achieve the vision you have of yourself in the future

Consider the types of assistance required to accomplish this. What types of connections would be most helpful to you? Do you have any acquaintances or relatives you would like to depend on or keep at a distance? Would consulting with a therapist or mentor assist you in working through your issues? Are there any additional professional resources available to you? Perhaps you'd also like to start improving your regular routine, behavior, or communication techniques.

Chapter Seven

Self Reflection

It is important to pause and reflect before releasing and transitioning from certain circumstances.

Effectively expressing the details of the situation, the insights you gained, the modifications you made, the specific aspects you wish to release, and the anticipated outcome of your decision can provide you with the necessary resources to implement your plan to let go.

To let go means to free oneself from any hesitation, apprehension, or anxiety regarding a circumstance, individual, or consequence.

The act of freeing yourself from anything that hinders your happiness and does not contribute to your progress.

Making the decision to let go entails choosing not to dwell on situations that are beyond your control and instead directing your attention to those you can manage.

Releasing the past creates room for new beginnings: freeing you from yesterday's events and unlocking opportunities for today's fresh possibilities.

Releasing involves embracing the present moment and ceasing to be anxious about the unknown future.

Simply claiming that you have released something is not sufficient; it requires a greater effort than that. For one to genuinely experience an improved state of being and proceed forth in a positive manner, a personal and internal transformation is required.

This year, I've been engaging in numerous dialogues with individuals and exploring various religious texts to gain insights on the art of releasing attachments. I've devised a set of five instructions that aid me in comprehending the process, and you might find them advantageous as well.

In a subtle manner, it is crucial that we acknowledge and respect our current progress in the process of relinquishing. This process may present greater difficulties for certain individuals compared to others. It is important to acknowledge that your current location is acceptable regardless of its specifics.

Enough Is Enough

By deliberately deciding to not allow past problems and individuals who caused us pain to dominate our thoughts, it is possible to break the pattern of dwelling on these negative thoughts, concepts, and emotions.

Your value is not determined by your thoughts. Your past experiences do not define you as a whole. Even if a situation fails, it does not define you as a failure or mean that you cannot achieve what you want in life.

As we detach our identity from our thoughts and just observe them passing by, it becomes simpler to release them.

Mental notions simply express mental ideas. Our actions towards those things have the power to either make us successful or lead to our downfall.

Emotionally Articulate

Being capable of articulating your emotions in a constructive manner is an additional measure towards analyzing and acknowledging them prior to releasing them. There are numerous discoveries that can be made by engaging in introspection. There are alternative methods to articulate your thoughts and feelings, such as confiding in a reliable confidant, loved one, or counselor. Occasionally, loved ones may be too emotionally invested in a specific circumstance to offer impartial assistance that aligns with your requirements. At times, their counsel may not be the most favorable. Letting go can be a difficult task at times. This holds even more weight when there are past recollections ingrained in your unconscious thoughts.

If we fail to fully process and resolve our past experiences of grief, anxiety, pain and resentment, they tend to accumulate and compound in our hearts, resulting in an even greater struggle to release and let go of them. If you find yourself in such a situation, it is crucial to receive therapy to address the underlying issues and recover thoroughly from within.

Reasoning

As humans, we are curious to understand the reasons behind the outcome of a situation and comprehend how an individual could inflict severe harm on us without considering the adverse effects on us.

We are of the opinion that we are entitled to receive the solutions to these queries. We require a certain degree of comprehension. Suffering lies in the fact that we often cannot attain the sense of finality we believe we deserve.

Not every person will offer an explanation for their actions or express regret when they are wrong. I have personal experience with how painful this truth can be. It feels as if a person is adding salt to an already painful injury.

It is unpleasant to proceed with life without a clear resolution, despite wanting satisfactory responses; however, this is a common occurrence for numerous individuals at some point in their lives.

The key to finding inner peace lies in wholeheartedly embracing the present circumstances and refraining from constantly yearning for change. This is the sole path towards achieving a state of contentment. This doesn't just pertain to acknowledging circumstances. It's imperative that we embrace individuals for their authentic selves and trust their actions to reveal their genuine nature. This is because they are telling the truth.

Letting Go And Moving On

Letting go and moving on often requires forgiving individuals who have not expressed remorse. Accepting an apology that may never be given is a necessity at times. It requires a great amount of fortitude, bravery, and modesty. Occasionally, the outcome may appear unjust and counterintuitive, but that is how circumstances may unfold.

It's a terrible feeling to harbor bitterness towards a person or situation for an extended period, while they gracefully progress in their life. Perpetrating this action solely causes harm to yourself as a matter of fact. Learning to forgive ourselves should take precedence.

One way to achieve this is by composing a letter addressed to yourself, in which you replace feelings of self-hatred with kindness, and resolve to opt for more positive decisions in the future.

Chapter Eight

Dwell On Good Things

Refusing to let go of one's pain does not result in any resolution. Continuously dwelling on the past cannot alter it, and merely desiring a different outcome does not create one.

At times, particularly with regard to historical events, one may have to acknowledge that they are clinging to a certain memory or idea, and then release it. This is how things transform. Releasing the source of your pain may seem like an insurmountable task, but it is necessary for your well-being.

If you choose to cling to the past, it can hinder your ability to establish a robust concept of yourself - a self that isn't shaped by your past, but rather by your desired identity. Surprisingly, distressing emotions may possess a sense of familiarity and ease, particularly when it is the only type of emotion one experiences. Certain individuals find it challenging to release their emotions of agony or discomfort related to their previous experiences because they believe these sentiments to be a fundamental aspect of their character. In certain aspects, their identity may be intertwined with their suffering in a way that they cannot separate themselves from it. This renders it impractical for them to release their grip.

Think On Your Daily Connections

Realize that the connections you anticipated having may not match the ones that actually materialize.

We need to acknowledge and embrace our present selves and also accept others just the way they are. As we progress through time, we consistently realize that events do not unfold according to our expectations - in fact, they rarely do. It's perfectly alright to acknowledge and examine your own actions in relationships, which can lead to enhancements. However, there may be occasions where you need to come to terms with the realities of certain individuals in your life. Develop a habit of expressing thankfulness, recognition and confidence in the journey.

A Vision

Realize that the connections you envisioned may not be identical to those you presently possess.

Avoid being too emotionally attached to the result when interacting with individuals, as this can frequently culminate in letdown.

Our expectations can hinder us as they can create a sense of anxiety towards specific results. There are no certainties in life, and we are powerless in influencing the results we hope to achieve when interacting with others. It is important to react in a logical and suitable manner when our desires or requirements are not fulfilled. At times, it entails establishing considerate limits while in other instances, relinquishing control may be necessary.

Realize that the connections you anticipated having may not align with the actual relationships you will form.

It is advisable to not attach too much importance to the end result while interacting with individuals, as it typically results in letdown.

You possess the key, so do not confine yourself. Our identity is often shaped by beliefs that hold us back and restrict our potential.

When we believe that we are incapable of achieving something, we hinder our chances of success. Therefore, it is essential to have confidence in oneself and one's abilities in order to attain one's objectives. Expand your thinking and have faith in your abilities. You will encounter countless individuals who will convey to you that it's beyond your capabilities. The responsibility lies with you to demonstrate their incorrectness.

Embrace the circumstances that are beyond your control.

Cease desiring for things to return to their former state. Get yourself to focus on the current moment. This is the place where life unfolds. The past cannot be altered, but present decisions can greatly influence the outcome of your future.

You will be able to unwind and savor the experience of living.

Articulation

Articulate what methods or approaches are effective for you.

Discover your unique perspective and communicate your thoughts and emotions in a logical manner to those around you. By consistently expressing what satisfies you and what doesn't, you'll avoid suppressing your feelings. Articulating oneself is a crucial aspect of experiencing positive emotions within oneself and fostering healthy connections with others.

Permit yourself to experience unfavorable feelings.

Respect your loss whether it's due to the passing away of a dear one or a separation. Suppressing your unfavorable emotions will prolong your agony. It can be a challenging task to cope with loss and it's completely acceptable to grant oneself permission to feel pain and sorrow. Allow your emotions to surface and experience the stages of grief in order to progress and advance.

An important takeaway for everyone is to strive towards releasing any obstacles that prevent one from truly experiencing oneself. You may come to the realization that others' opinions of you do not define your true identity. Your identity is not defined by your pain, past experiences, or emotions. Our aspirations for self-improvement are hindered by the harmful self-criticism and negative beliefs we hold about ourselves. Releasing things necessitates a firm understanding of oneself, empowering you to gain insight and progress from life events.

Chapter Nine

Simple Skills To Help

- Learn a new skill instead of dwelling on the skills you never mastered
- Alter your viewpoint and regard the underlying issue as a disguised opportunity to improve who you are
- Its okay to cry if you have to. Releasing your negative emotions through tears can help eliminate the harmful chemicals that accumulate in your body as a result of stress.
- Let it all out. Expressing unpleasant emotions via weeping helps your body rid itself of dangerous substances that have accumulated as a result of stress.
- Transform your dissatisfaction into an urgent, constructive action. For example, you may head to the community center to volunteer or make some calls about new career options.
- Instead of concentrating on the past or worrying about the future, use meditation or yoga to bring you into the present.
- Create a list of all of your successes, no matter how minor, and add to it every day. To make room for this

self-satisfaction, you'll need to let go of a little dissatisfaction.
- Focus on expanding your ability set rather than ruminating on the
- Be willing to give up some control, you will find some degree of calm. When you let go of a lot of things, you'll find that you have a lot more peace.
- The reason people have created and kept is because they offer a sense of they we are as individuals. Perhaps this helps to explain why they often cling to their suffering long after it has outlived its usefulness to us. NO LONGER ALONG NEGATIVE MEMORIES, NEGATIVE THOUGHTS TO BE A PART OF WHO YOU ARE. LET IT GO.
- Behaviors in the here and now are influenced by sentiments of embarrassment and regret, which are triggered when we mentally relive previous errors over and over again. JUST SAY WHEN. KNOW WHEN TO LET THE PAST GO. Holing on to annoyance and concern about the future as though the act of fixating on these things gives us some kind of control over them. THINK WELL OF THE FUTURE, BUT LIVE IN THE MOMENT. We assume that being in a state of tension is the usual, even though it may lead to major health problems because we store stress in both our thoughts and our bodies. FIX YOUR PERSPECTIVE ON GOOD THINGS.
- Every second is a new opportunity to let go and experience a sense of calm. The following are some

options for getting started. Release Your Frustration with Yourself and Your Life and Move On. Focus on expanding your ability set rather than ruminating on the abilities you've yet to fully develop.

- Adjust your perspective and look at the underlying problem as an opportunity hidden in plain sight.
- Let out a good scream. Allowing yourself to scream out your unpleasant emotions allows your body to rid itself of dangerous chemicals that have accumulated as a result of stress.
- Channel your dissatisfaction into an instant constructive activity, such as walking to the local community center to volunteer or making some phone calls to inquire about new career options.
- Instead of ruminating on the events of the past or being anxious about the future, try meditating or practicing yoga to help you become more present in the here and now.
- Compile a list of all of your achievements, no matter how little they may seem, and add to it every day. You are going to have to let go of some of your unhappiness in order to create room for this feeling of self-satisfaction.
- Conjure up a mental container and give it the name "Expectations." If you find yourself ruminating on how things ought to be or ought to have been, make a mental note to file those thoughts away in this container.

- Participate in some kind of physical exercise. Endorphins are molecules that boost your state of mind and exercise has been shown to lower levels of stress hormones in the body.
- Instead of ruminating on the things that you can't change, concentrate all of your attention into improving the things that you can change.
- Use a creative outlet, such as writing or painting, to express the emotions that you're experiencing. Put this on your list of things to do, and then check it off after it's finished. This will serve as a visible reminder that you have consciously made the decision to let go of these emotions.
- Allow yourself some time to vent your frustrations. Before approaching the individual who has been bothering you, give yourself a day to express your frustrations. It is possible that this may defuse the antagonism and allow you time to arrange a confrontation that is sensible.
- Remind yourself that your anger hurts you more than the person who offended you, and as an act of compassion to yourself, envision your anger dissipating as a method to get rid of it.
- If you are able to do so, voice your outrage directly to the individual who has wronged you. It's possible that expressing how you feel can help you move on. You should keep in mind that you do not have any influence on how the offender reacts; the only thing

you can influence is how clearly and politely you explain yourself.

- Admit that you are responsible. When you're upset, you tend to fixate on what the other person did that was wrong, which, in essence, takes away your authority. Many people experience a sense of empowerment and a reduction in bitterness when they reflect on what they might have done differently.
- Put yourself in the position of the guilty party. We are all fallible, and there is a good chance that you, your spouse, your father, or a friend could have easily made the same error as you did. Compassion is the antidote to rage.
- Literally and figuratively discard it. Try going on a jog while carrying a bag full of tennis balls, for instance. After you've worked up a bit of a sweat, start tossing the balls one at a time while identifying each one as a different aspect of your rage. (You will need to rescue them since trash is offensive to the environment!)
- Make use of a stress ball, and while you're doing so, verbalize and physically show your frustration while doing so. Make a face like you're about to snarl or groan. Even if you may think you sound ridiculous, doing so enables you to communicate exactly how you are feeling on the inside.
- Remind yourself that the only choices you have are to remove yourself from the circumstance, attempt to alter the situation, or accept the situation as it is.

These actions provide enjoyment, however hanging on to resentment will never do so.

- Release Your Attachment to Your Past Relationships. Determine what you learned from the event to assist you in developing a feeling of closure.
- Put all you want to say into writing and send it in a letter. Even if you decide not to send it, elaborating on your emotions can assist you in coming to grips with the present state of affairs more effectively.
- Imagine yourself as a strong and independent single person—the person you were before you met your most recent partner. That other person was fairly amazing, and now you have the opportunity to step into their shoes once again.
- Create an environment that is reflective of your current state of being.
- Pin up this reminder in a place where you can easily notice it. "Loving myself requires that I let go of things."
- Rather of thinking emotionally, focus on the facts instead. Don't try to fight the emotion that comes over you when you think, "I'll never feel loved again!" Change your train of thinking to something else, such as "I learned a new song for karaoke tonight."
- Employ the method of talking in a goofy voice. Changing the voice in your brain to that of a cartoon character as a way to reclaim some of the authority that the troublesome notion has taken from you.

- Let Go Of Stress . To calm yourself and bring your attention into the here and now, try practicing a deep breathing technique.
- Participate actively in an activity that involves other people. Taking time to appreciate the individuals you have in your life may make it easier to put your issues into perspective.
- Let go of it in a figurative sense. Put everything that's stressing you out on paper, and then burn it all in the fireplace.
- Substitute new ideas with old ones. If you are aware of when you start thinking about something that causes you tension, you will be able to redirect your thought process to something more pleasurable, such as the enjoyment you get from your activity.
- Visualize what your life will be like in 10 years from now. Then consider the future twenty years from now, and then thirty years from now. You need to come to terms with the fact that many of the things that are causing you anxiety do not actually important in the larger scheme of things.
- Organize your desk. Doing a simple activity both boosts your perception that you are in charge of the situation and lowers your overall stress level.
- Create two lists: one with the factors that are contributing to your stress, and another with the steps you can take to remedy those factors. Imagine that you are using up and running out of your "stress

supply" as you go through each step of completing these activities.

- Just try to laugh it off. Laughing can reduce stress, boost your immune system, and even make pain more bearable. If you find that you are unable to relax for an extended period of time, try starting with only ten minutes of viewing an amusing video on YouTube.

Chapter Ten

Controlling Emotions

Anxiety, panic attacks, overpowering emotions, negative thoughts, pain, or emotional triggers are some of the conditions that may benefit from distraction as a coping method. It is important to know what distraction is, how it may be used as a form of coping, how it functions, and different techniques to divert oneself.

If you were raised by parents who were abusive, you probably struggle with a good deal of what was discussed earlier in this article.

It's possible that you have a lot of anxious thoughts or negative thoughts, which often send you into a tailspin of fear or pessimism. It's possible that you, like me, are quickly triggered, which might result in sensations, thoughts, and emotional memories that are overpowering.

When faced with a situation like that, you could feel the want to resort to whatever means necessary in order to put an end to such feelings and ideas. However, when you reach this point, you run the danger of turning to unhealthy coping mechanisms that may end up causing you much more harm. I'm quite sure that I've been there before.

This is where the problem of distraction arises.

The Power Of Distractions

A distraction is something you do to momentarily divert your attention away from another topic or activity.

In the context of mental health, a mental health "distraction" refers to anything that might momentarily divert your attention away from an unpleasant experience, such as a strong emotion, a worrisome idea, or the sensations of physical pain. In addition to that, a lot of people utilize it to stop ruminating.

It is essential to keep in mind that distraction is not synonymous with avoidance or numbness.

Avoidance prevents you from confronting your feelings as well as your difficulties. As a result, your feelings become less intense.

Distraction, on the other hand, removes you temporarily from the cause of your misery with the intention that you will return at a later time to process it. Therefore, it is essential to keep in mind that using a distraction of any kind as a coping method is just a short-term solution.

A distraction offers you space, which enables you to relax down and put yourself in a better mental state to deal with the issue at hand when it has passed. It is important that you continue to provide yourself with the necessary amount of emotional care once you are in a position where you can do it more easily.

The purpose of distraction is to keep you safe in the here and now by avoiding harmful actions that can emerge as a reaction to overpowering sensations or ideas that come up.

It also helps delay having to deal with your emotions, which is helpful if they are too overwhelming at the present or if they are occurring at an inconvenient time or location.

Additionally, while you are in a negative frame of mind, it may be difficult for you to think about the issue in an impartial manner. You may exaggerate the severity of those bad sentiments or concentrate on them, both of which may make those feelings more intense.

In circumstances such as these, you could feel the temptation to resort to unhealthier coping techniques in an effort to swiftly improve how you feel about your situation.

Although such strategies could at first be able to alleviate the overwhelming sensations, the relief they provide is only brief. On the contrary, in the long term it will lead to an increase in both the number of difficulties and the intensity of the feelings experienced.

In light of the above, it is essential to address your feelings as they arise; but, there are other instances in which your feelings may be so taxing that you need to take a moment to compose yourself before confronting them.

By diverting your attention elsewhere for a little while, you buy yourself some time to let the feeling pass, which makes it much simpler to deal with after the fact.

Engaging in activities that temporarily divert one's attention away from a problematic subject may be beneficial for managing the feelings that are associated with conditions such as anxiety, PTSD, and depression. Additionally, it seems to be beneficial for both acute and chronic pain.

In order for distraction to be effective, you must first be able to detect when you are experiencing overwhelming thoughts or feelings. You should make an effort to recognize warning indicators such as the want to hide, run away, isolate yourself, or damage yourself.

It may be difficult to prevent oneself from experiencing certain feelings or thinking particular ideas, but you should at least make an effort to be aware of when this is occurring.

Then, as soon as you become aware of it, immediately begin engaging in an activity that will serve as a distraction for you, regardless of whether or not you feel like it or believe it will be of any use. At the very least, give it five minutes of your attention before you move on to another method of diverting your attention.

Depending on the conditions, you may divert yourself for anywhere from a few minutes and a few days at a time. But please keep in mind that you will ultimately need to give yourself the emotional attention you need in order to move through whatever it is that you are having trouble with.

How To Distract Yourself

If you want to be able to employ distraction, you should prepare yourself by having a few different strategies to divert your attention on hand and ready to go when the time comes.

Take a look at this list of over the various strategies that you may use to divert yourself anytime powerful emotions, bad thoughts, pain, or anything else that is too much to cope with arises. You can use any one of these methods whenever you feel the need to.

While you are going through the list, jot down any distraction suggestions that you think may be useful to you. The more items you include on your list, the less difficult it will be to find anything to divert your attention to when the appropriate moment arrives.

This contributes to the overall effectiveness of the distraction. It also makes it less likely that you would deal with a strategy that is bad for you.

Before we go any further, could you kindly acknowledge that each person is unique? It's possible that a diversionary activity that helps someone else may not do the trick for you, and vice versa. For instance, you could find that particular activities, either at certain times or more generally, might be triggering for you.

In addition, as you continue down this list, keep in mind that certain circumstances may prevent you from engaging in some of the activities on it.

For instance, if you are working, it is quite unlikely that you will be able to go for a run or play video games. In such situation, it's possible that more straightforward mental exercises might be more beneficial. Reading articles or scrolling through social media doesn't seem like it would be a good idea if you are feeling especially concerned about the news.

Therefore, you should attempt to think of the many scenarios in which you will need to employ these methods to divert yourself. You should also feel free to think up more techniques on your own as you go through the list.

- Begin with a huge number and count down in reverse (999, 998, 997)
- Pick a number to begin with, and then continue adding numbers to it (15 + 7 = 22, 22 + 7 = 29, etc.).
- Pick a number, such as 10, and consider the many permutations that may be used to arrive at that number.
- Make a tally of how many of whatever there is in your immediate surroundings (how many objects are blue? How many objects that are round?)
- Recognize each and every hue present in the space.
- Learn to commit to memory and bring to mind all you observe in this room.
- Choose a topic from anything that comes to mind and try to list as many items in that topic as you can (for example, nations, fruits, animals). You may make it more difficult by listing items in alphabetical order from A to Z or by using the final letter of the previous word as the first letter of the new word you construct.
- You might recite a paragraph, song, poetry, or anything else that you are familiar with.

- Describe to yourself precisely what it is that you are doing at this very minute.
- If you don't already have one, establish a mantra and keep repeating it to yourself. ('I'm capable of handling this', 'This too will pass') Spell it out in its entirety if just repetition is not sufficient.
- Consider doing a typical job in the order that it should be done. Imagine that you are providing instruction to another person on how to do the task.
- Observe something and provide a very detailed description of it. Take note of how it appears, the pattern it has, the texture it has, and how it feels. (This apple is green overall, and there are two little bruises on it...)
- The home has to be cleaned (including sweeping, vacuuming, and wiping down the windows, etc.).
- Do the dishes.
- Scrub the bathtubs, commodes, and sinks.
- Wash your automobile
- Take care of the yard.
- Cut the grass and do the wash.
- Ensure that filters are clean.
- Check to see that everything is operating normally.
- Perform any necessary maintenance or be trained to do so.
- Do a digital declutter for your gadgets, emails, and social media
- Everything should be organized online.

- Getting rid of clutter (in the house, the room, the closet, the vehicle, the garage, etc.)
- Items, such books, the kitchen, the pantry, the bathroom, and the desk, need to be reorganized.
- Sort through the many pieces of paper (mail, documents, paperwork, etc.).
- Make sure that your meals are pre-planned.
- Shop for groceries
- Compile a list of your objectives.
- Get your old movies and pictures in order.
- Put your fiscal house in order.
- Make a financial plan
- Develop a strategy for your finances.
- Start getting things done that you have been putting off.
- Make a strategy for unexpected events.
- Digitize critical papers
- Make an inventory of your possessions for the purpose of obtaining insurance.
- Develop, update, renew, or amend legal documents
- Figure out some innovative methods to save costs.
- Look for any helpful software or an application that you can utilize.
- Start your holiday shopping early.
- Plan for a future trip
- Obtaining a license or other kind of certification
- Attend some classes.
- Participate in a discussion group or a seminar.
- Acquire a second language.

- Master the skills necessary to play an instrument.
- Acquire more information about various technological aspects.
- Acquire the skills necessary to cut your own hair.
- Check out a few TED Talks.
- Master the art of sewing.
- Acquire some fresh expertise.
- Despite what you're doing—driving, cleaning your teeth, doing dishes, or working out—you may apply the mindfulness practice to any of these activities. The point is to pay attention to the here and now.
- Meditate
- Engage in some deep breathing exercises.
- Make use of some guided images.
- Carry out the practice of the body check.
- Find novel ways to do things: It is possible to prevent old thinking patterns from reoccurring by replacing them with new ones and diverting your attention away from the previous ones.
- Make sure that you have a place where you can go to unwind, work, meditate, or be creative. Make it your own personal area.
- Journal
- Unplug: Take a break from all of your electronic gadgets once in a while.
- Put a stop to the nastiness online: If a page or community seems to be spreading negativity, you should either block, remove, or unfollow it.
- Develop a schedule for your workouts.

- Learn how to compete in a sport.
- Go out for a jog.
- Take a wander outdoors
- Go stargazing
- Jumprope
- Practice yoga
- Go cycling
- Go camping
- Weightlifting
- Get in touch with nature.
- Take a relaxing soak in the tub.
- Have a relaxing soak in the tub.
- Stretch
- Get a therapeutic massage.
- Have a spa day
- Get a face
- Do some self-care and get a manicure or pedicure.
- Play some music that will calm you down.
- Something should be read, watched, or played.
- Take a warm bath
- Make over your appearance for yourself.
- Get dressed up
- Do something pleasant for yourself every once in a while.
- Paint or sketch
- Put some paint on it.
- You may try sketching the contours blind.
- Build a model
- Coloring

- Create a sculpture out of clay, dough, or aluminum foil.
- The art of fashion design
- Create a brand image
- Make songs
- Engage in some kind of creative activity.
- Give photography a go.
- Make adjustments to pictures using Photoshop.
- Master the art of calligraphy.
- Write
- Make progress on a book.
- Create some verse or a short tale.
- Create a weblog.
- Making basic works of art and crafts using craft kits or items found about the house
- Try your hand at some paper art
- Repurpose something else
- Construct a home for the local avifauna.
- Do a DIY project
- Modify something
- Make a drawing of your house or the area around it.
- Put together a scrapbook.
- Give things a unique touch.
- Make jewelry
- Create decorations for the impending occasion, season, or holiday you have coming up.
- Draw your ideal house
- Create an uplifting poster for others.
- Create something new.

- Create your own homemade beauty or cleaning product.
- Start gardening.
- Grow anything from seed.
- Produce candles.
- Do nail designs
- Design a design for a tattoo
- Experiment with your hair in various ways.
- Something has to be redecorated.
- reorganize the furnishings in your house.
- Make videos
- Create an animation using stop-motion techniques.
- Start a new creative pastime now.
- Try your hand at some crocheting, knitting, or embroidery.
- Try woodworking or metalwork
- Create some get-well-soon cards.
- Cook or bake something
- Decorate desserts
- Experiment with a new dish's recipe.
- Recreate a recipe you like and play around with the components you already have at home.
- Experiment with a variety of various combinations of foods.
- Blend some fruit together.
- Create a culinary demonstration or instructional video.
- Create an ancestor chart.
- Create a capsule to hold time.
- Create a memorable picture book for your family.

- Create comic books.
- Spend some time shopping, even if it's simply looking at storefront windows.
- Spend some time reading a book, a short story, or a poem.
- Take part in a game on your mobile device.
- Take in some entertainment, such as a film, program on television, reality show, food show, or documentary.
- YouTube watching till you puke
- Take a look at some commercials or music videos.
- View sporting events.
- Explore new musical territory.
- Play video games
- You may engage in a card game by yourself or with another player.
- Explore several blogs and see what catches your eye.
- Read some blog entries
- Listen to a podcast
- Create checklists of things you want to read, watch, do, listen to, play, etc.
- Place items in order (the finest 10 movies, the top 5 musical acts, the best 5 cuisines, etc.).
- Create separate playlists of music for different situations, including tracks for dancing, music for resting, bops, and so on.
- Talk to someone about what you've been watching, reading, or playing.
- Explore the various social media.

- Look at cartoons
- Listen to tunes
- Sing or do karaoke
- Dance
- Engage your mind with these online games.
- Host a get-together
- Enjoy some quality time with your pet.
- You should show your pet some new skills.
- Participate in a photograph with your animal companion.
- Do some digging into your family tree.
- Take a few pictures
- Commence a collection of...
- Make parodies
- Create a glowing testimonial for something you found enjoyable.
- Acquire an understanding of a culture
- Explore Wiki
- Watch a movie or play from another country.
- Attend anime shows.
- Take in some comics or graphic novels.
- Make a bucket list
- Create a game
- Explore the natural world.
- Have a look around virtually.
- Attend a virtual concert
- Explore every corner of the globe with Google Earth.
- Read a few jokes

- Read articles that pertain to the topics that interest you.
- Participate in some goofy online quizzes.
- Do a jigsaw puzzle
- Compete in Scrabble.
- Try your hand at a crossword or a word search.
- Take part in a simple word game.
- Participate in a game of memory.
- Do Sudoku tasks
- Get caught up on the most recent happenings.
- Learn more about some of your favorite famous people.
- Go to a virtual escape room
- Attend a virtual event
- Get in touch with a loved one by phone call, text message, or video chat.
- Set a time to get together with your friends to do something fun like bowling, see a movie, or get a cup of coffee.
- Spend time with a friend or family member, either in person or digitally.
- Send a letter to a member of your family or a close friend.
- Talk to an unknown person through the internet.
- Participate in a community on the internet.
- Join a support group
- Volunteer
- Take part in a conversation on the internet that piques your curiosity.

- Attend an improv workshop.
- Participate in a club.
- Participate in a game with another person online.
- Watch anything along with another person online.
- Experience the thrill of a virtual world.
- Pay a visit to the community center in your area.
- Take part in the activities of the religious organization that is closest to you.
- Put together a care box or present for a friend or loved one.

Chapter Eleven

Letting People Go

Having to part ways with someone you care about is perhaps the most difficult thing to do. It's possible that you're ending a romantic connection, but it's also possible that you're ending a friendship. Both of these things may be difficult. It may be difficult to move on from a relationship, whether you are doing so because the other person is no longer a part of your life or because you have made the conscious decision to exclude this person from your future plans.

Have positive expectations.

When letting go, it is helpful to think about the positive things that will occur in the future and to have an optimistic outlook on the situation. If we anticipate that we would fail, we are more likely to do so.

Refrain From Assigning Blame

When we place blame on another person, we are making assumptions about the motivations behind what they have done. Perhaps we have the misconception that they were maliciously nasty to us with the objective of causing us pain. However, it is impossible for us to know the motivations of other people, and laying blame on them keeps us trapped wishing that the other person had behaved differently rather than teaching us how to behave differently in the future so that we may more successfully achieve our goals.

Be kind and compassionate to yourself.

Self-compassion is a practice that may be helpful in healing wounds and facilitating successful onward movement, regardless of who made the decision to let go of whom. Therefore, make an effort to be kind to yourself, forgive yourself for whatever errors you've made, and acknowledge your requirements just as they are.

Letting Go of Angry Feelings

When we have trouble letting go of anger, it's a sign that we're having a hard time moving on from something that occurred in the past. Perhaps we have been wronged, mistreated, or taken advantage of, all of which are perfectly reasonable reasons to feel furious about the situation. However, harboring resentment may cause us to develop difficulties related to rage and prevent us from appreciating what is happening in the here and now.

Let Go Of Inflexible Beliefs

When we are angry, we often adopt hostile, resentful, or suspicious attitudes toward others. When our viewpoints and notions of what constitutes good and evil are challenged by the world around us, we find ourselves experiencing feelings of rage. If we can merely relax our adherence to our views and acknowledge that the events, perspectives, and behaviors experienced by other people are valid, then we will have a lot less cause for resentment in our lives.

Channel Your Rage Into Productive Action

Anger is a bad feeling that may give you a boost of energy. It is possible that repressing it will be harmful to our health. Rage may cause us to have a better feeling of power and control over our life if we use it to restore justice, respect, and relational reciprocity.

Getting Rid Of Fear

If we are unable to let go of our fears, it is likely because we are hanging on to concerns about the potential outcomes of certain events in the future. It's conceivable that we just can't stop picturing the worst that may happen. Perhaps we are placing an undue amount of emphasis on the potential negative outcomes rather than considering the positive possibilities. Or maybe we are anxious about anything in particular that we are aware has in store for us in the future. Whatever it is that you have reason to be afraid about, excessive worrying is a waste of energy. Because we waste our time worrying about things that may or may not even happen the way we anticipate they will, we lose out on the wonderful things that are taking place now at this very moment. So in order to assist you overcome your fears, here are some pointers:

Practice Appreciation

We may direct our attention, in addition to changing our focus to potentially positive developments in our future, to the positive developments that are occurring in our present. When we are in our minds, dwelling on the terrible things that are yet to come, we fail to see the pleasant things that are occurring in the here and now. So make an effort to take a look at the world around you and think of a few things for which you are thankful.

Give Journaling A TRY

Think about jotting down a list of all the things that scare you. Once you have them written down, you may make a conscious decision to stop thinking about them beyond that point. You can always go back and look at them if you feel the need to, but the amazing thing is that you usually don't—you've let them go. You have the option to do either one of these things at any time.

Let Go and Relax

Because letting go includes making a mental shift — moving from being connected to something to being okay with that object no longer being in our lives — it essentially entails dealing with our ideas and mental processes. This shift involves moving from being attached to something to being alright with that something no longer being a part of our lives. Mindfulness meditation is one method that may be used to help us deal with our thoughts and develop a deeper capacity for acceptance.

The practice of mindfulness entails paying attention to one's internal and external events in a manner that is welcoming, free of judgment, and unattached. Practicing mindfulness meditation may make it easier for us to let go of unhelpful ideas. We may possibly improve our ability to let go and make it easier for ourselves to let go in our day-to-day lives if we regularly engage in the practice of letting go of our thoughts and emotions.

Meditation can help you let go, as taught in this video.

Give Some Thought To Whether Or Not You Are Prepared To Let Go.

Ask yourself some introspective questions to determine whether or not you are really prepared to let go. Is this person or this event going to end up hurting you more than it will help you? Do you sense a tug in the other direction, away from this person or experience? Or do you get the impression that you have to remain here and keep working toward the goal of making this aspect of your life better?

It's important to recognize that in today's world of fast food, swipe left, and never-ending alternatives, it's simpler than ever for us to give up on things too quickly than it was in the past. It's possible that we may choose to let go rather than put in the effort required to correct something that should be fixed. Therefore, give yourself as much time as you need to thoroughly consider the options.

Figure Out What Is Preventing You From Letting Go Of The Situation.

If you've made it this far in the post, it's probable that you've been giving letting go some thought for quite some time. What exactly has been holding you back? Are you unsure? Are you afraid? Are you unsure of what the next measures are that need to be taken? It is perfectly OK to hold on to something until the moment comes when you can do it with peace of mind.

To give you an example, let's say you know for certain that it's time for you to quit a job, but you're still undecided about what kind of work you want to do in the future. Before taking the first step, it is acceptable to put some effort into determining the next move to do. Do what makes sense to you, and take as much time as you need to do it.

Develop A Strategy For 'Letting Go' Of Your Past

If you are at a point in your life where you are ready to let go, make the choice to do so, commit to that decision, and devise a strategy for how you will carry it out. What are the specific steps that you intend to take? When do you plan to pick them up? How do you plan to get beyond the potential obstacles that arise when you let go? If you can make your strategy as clear as possible, putting it into action will be much simpler.

Below is a list of other techniques that you may find helpful in letting go of the past and learning the ability of letting go.

1. Notice resistance. Pay attention to any feelings of resistance that you have while trying to let go. What does it reveal about who you are and the things that you desire?

2. Question your patterns. Do you feel that letting go of things is difficult for you on a regular basis? Or, do you have a hard time letting go of a certain object or person in your life? What exactly are these patterns, and how exactly are they either serving you or working against you?

3. Talk to the kid inside you. As we become older, we tend to make judgments based more on the logic and reasoning in our heads, rather than on our feelings or our gut instincts. Whenever you find yourself debating whether or not to let go of anything, take a moment to stop and inquire about the desires of your inner child. Examine the responses you are given to see if they may provide you with any previously undiscovered insights.

4. Recognize that our expectations are not always in line with reality. Television and movies often provide a false perspective of what real-life relationships are like as well as the experience of living in general. Growing up, the majority of us have the idea and the expectation that things would be different than they really are. And once we

are aware of the truth, we struggle against it. If you
recognize yourself in this description, you should make an
effort to let go of the ideals you formerly had and replace
them with the truth as you know it today.

Chapter Twelve

Try Practicing Mindfulness Via Meditation

Learning how to quit ruminating on things that bring you discomfort is one of the many benefits that may come from practicing meditation. People may find it easier to be present in the moment and become more at ease with themselves as a result. You are able to sit quietly without being disturbed and concentrate on your breathing when you practice mindfulness meditation. Listen, concentrate on how you feel, and pay attention to each inhale and exhale. It is possible that other ideas may enter your brain while you are doing this, and when they do, you should make an effort to just let them go without passing judgment on them and return your attention to your breath. Learning to let ideas go rather than following them is a skill that may be improved by doing the activity described here.

Meditation teaches one to pay attention to the here and now, rather than becoming caught up in one's thoughts or worrying about the future or the past. You are able to notice the idea as it occurs to you and accept the fact that you are thinking about it at that moment. The next step is to become aware that the idea is dissipating like a cloud and to redirect one's attention to the feeling of breathing in and out. If you do this, you will be able to utilize this approach outside of the time that is specifically set out for formal meditation in order to calm down, focus on your breathing, and determine whether or not anything that is upsetting you is something that is worth focusing your attention on. If you feel that it is simpler to begin practicing under the direction of a teacher, there are a lot of different guided mindfulness exercises that you can do online that are free of charge.

Make An Effort To Reduce The Amount You Complain

Complaining may be a normal reaction to feeling upset, but talking about an issue excessively does not always genuinely help you. Complaining can be a natural response to feeling upset. Complaining, on the other hand, is an activity that encourages your mind to remain anxious about the past or the future. Mindfulness entails paying attention to the time at hand, but complaining, on the other hand, involves paying attention to the moment at hand. Complaining has the potential to amplify an issue, making it seem much more significant than it really is. However, it is a pattern of behavior that, with enough work, you may learn to regulate.

For example, if you have ever been cut off while driving, you understand how frightening and frustrating the experience can be. When something like this occurs, it's easy to feel tempted to whine about it to other people and let it completely spoil your day. But doing so gives the frustration more force than it ought to have, while at the same time contributing nothing to the resolution of the problem. Instead, make an effort to realize the fleeting nature of the irritation, acknowledge the feelings you are experiencing, and then let go of those feelings so that you may go on.

things go under your skin?

Try to Gain Some Perspective on the Things That Are Stressing You Out.

When you discover that you are dwelling on a certain topic for an extended period of time, it might be good to engage in a mental exercise in which you ask yourself, "What is the most likely thing that can happen?" Then carry that line of reasoning all the way through to its illogical conclusion. It's possible that you'll come to the realization that no matter what does occur, you'll be able to go through it.

When someone is worried, their mind tends to fixate on the worst case situation.

It is essential to bear in mind that until you really go through the experience, you will not be able to know what the true outcome will be. Recognize that the anxieties you are feeling are the result of a notion that you have been building in your brain about something that may or may not happen, rather than something that will really happen. In addition to this, it could be helpful to ask yourself questions like, "How big of an impact will this have on me tomorrow? What about in twelve months from now?" This may help put the passing of a few seconds or minutes into better perspective.

Let Go Of The Controls

It's easy to get caught up in overthinking things that aren't actually within our control the majority of the time. If we can learn to accept the things that we cannot change and work on changing the things that we can, we will be able to make a significant amount of headspace available to us and experience a greater sense of peace. We are not always able to modify or control the unpredictable occurrences that occur in life or the actions of other people. We have the ability to alter our responses and reactions to these situations; so, rather than concentrating inwardly on things that are beyond our control, we should strive to let go of anxiety and instead concentrate on things that are within our sphere of influence.

A few ladies conversing while seated at a table.

Description mechanically created with just a little bit of trust

Are You Struggling To Let Things Go?

If there are times when you feel like you simply can't let anything go, one option for getting assistance is to go to a qualified counselor. Working with a counselor may assist you in developing new methods and instruments for achieving a higher level of well-being.

If you discover that you regularly encounter unsettling ideas or feelings, you may find it beneficial to reach out to your therapist at those times when you find yourself having these thoughts. If you are participating in online therapy with BetterHelp, you will have the ability to message your therapist whenever you want inside the application, and they will get back to you as soon as they can.

It has been shown that online therapy is useful for a variety of issues, including mental diseases such as anxiety and depression, which might entail thoughts that are upsetting to the patient. For instance, researchers conducted a comprehensive assessment of the literature to investigate the efficacy of internet-based cognitive behavioral therapy (ICBT) for treating a variety of mental diseases. The study came to the conclusion that "ICBT is effective in the treatment and management of various psychiatric disorders such as depression, social anxiety, panic disorders," and a number of other conditions.

Chapter Thirteen

Learning how to let things go is much easier said than done. In so many cases, we know we need to let go so we can move on to happier times, but the act of letting go is extremely difficult.

Whether you need to let go of a bad relationship, a toxic work situation, a lost dream, an argument there are steps you can take that will help you let go in a way that doesn't seem overwhelming.

The steps I'm sharing below are what I've worked through to help me let go of my own personal lost dream – having a biological baby of my own.

These tips are helpful no matter what your situation is and I hope you'll find them practical and effective to help you move on.

Why Letting Go Is So Important

When you're holding on to something that isn't working or you're in a place in your life that disrupts your happiness, you are essentially halting good things from entering your life.

Letting go means you can:

- Focus on having a new beginning and moving forward
- Prioritize gratitude in your life
- Have healthier relationships and forgive those who matter
- Decrease stress and anxiety
- Concentrate on the positive things in life
- Sleep better at night
- Decrease ruminating thoughts and negative thoughts

Feel Your Feelings

Understand that it's okay to feel everything you need to feel. The first step in letting things go is giving yourself permission to truly feel.

Be present with your uncomfortable or negative feelings. Notice when painful feelings arise.

This helps you understand painful experiences, validates them and gives you a different perspective.

Don't feel guilty or become angry with yourself for how you feel.

Accept your feelings and know that you are allowed to FEEL it all.

Think About Why It's Important For You To Let Go

Knowing why it's important to let go of the past or let go of some of the hardest things you've experienced will help you with the process of letting go.

Ask yourself:

- If you let go of this feeling, person or situation how will this make you feel?
- How will letting go improve your daily life right now? What great things will you have more mind space for?
- What will there be room for if you let go?
- How does letting go support your value system?

During this process also think about the harmful effects of holding on.

Imagine Life Once You've Let Go

Now that you've thought about your why, I want you to imagine life without this 'thing' you're holding on to.

Ask yourself:

- What will you be able to focus on instead? A family member you want to support? A healthy relationship?
- How will your time be spent differently instead of the stress and worry of holding on? Perhaps you can spend more time on personal growth, self care, self love?

Have a Backup Feel Better Plan

Once you begin to take action on letting go of a situation, feeling or person you need to have a backup feel better plan.

What is this?

A feel better plan is a list of activities you do when you feel yourself about to digress.

To create a feel better plan, start by writing a list of things you can do to feel better immediately. Examples include:

- Walking the dog
- Playing music
- Calling your best friend
- Knocking on your neighbour's door
- Eating chocolate
- Deep breathing

This list will be unique to you and the point is when you feel yourself falling backward towards upset do something off your list.

Distance Yourself

Distance yourself from people, places or situations that make letting go hard to do.

For example, If you're trying to let go of a relationship don't go to the neighborhood your ex lives in. Or, if you're trying to move on from something like infertility, don't attend your cousin's baby shower. Distancing yourself from things that hurt is designed for you to look after yourself.

Focus on Acceptance

Depending on the situation, letting go can be extremely difficult, especially if you're the type of person who likes (and needs) to be in control.

When you can't control a situation the only choice you have is to eventually let go. This is important for your overall well-being and mental health.

How do you accept something?

I highly encourage you to focus a gratitude practice.

Use a gratitude journal. Write a gratitude list. Write down 3 things you're grateful for every single day. Try this 30 day gratitude challenge

Focusing on gratitude will help you see all of the wonderful things you have in your life today, which in turn makes the process of accepting that you have to move on that much easier.

Learn How To Love Yourself

Loving yourself isn't selfish, it's necessary. The more you do this the easier it will be to let go of things that are taking up your precious time, energy and mental space.

Once you honestly love and care for yourself, you'll find that letting go is actually much easier. Why? Because holding on to something that isn't going to change is unhealthy for you.

Chapter Fourteen

Be A Better You

Everyone strives to be the greatest version of themselves, but many people question whether or not it is really possible to improve as a person after they have reached adulthood. The answer is unequivocally and unequivocally yes. There is never a point in time when one has reached their full potential. Nevertheless, this response brings up even more inquiries.

How can you grow as a person such that you become a better version of yourself? What is the most straightforward method? And what would you say are the most vital components of one's personality to develop? Here are some of the most significant things you can do to improve yourself as a person, taking into consideration not just your personal well-being but also the best interests of others.

Control Yourself

We all, at some point in our life, have felt the sting of rage. However, if we do not learn to regulate our anger, it may negatively impact not just our relationships but also our health.1 All of this may result in more stress and new challenges, which makes life more difficult and prevents us from becoming the greatest versions of ourselves. To become a better person, it is critical to acquire the skills necessary to first control and then gradually let go of one's anger.

It is not always simple to be able to let go of one's anger. The first thing you need to do, though, is educate yourself on how to identify anger and become familiar with appropriate responses to situations in which you feel furious.

If you make an effort to recognize when you feel angry and decide to handle this emotion rather than rejecting it or lashing out at others as a method of coping, recognizing anger is generally a straightforward process that can be done with little effort on your part. Your goal should be to become more aware of when and why you experience anger, and to be aware that there is a distinction between experiencing anger and acting on that anger. Then, be familiar with your choices.

You have the ability to adjust the beliefs you have about the things that are irritating you. This may help if you discover more about the scenario, or even if you just remind yourself that there are probably still things going on that you aren't aware of.

Bring to mind the possibility that the driver who cut you off in traffic was maybe preoccupied with a difficult situation in their own life and just forgot to yield to you. Ask your buddy about how their day is going and find out if there is anything more that you don't know about them if they appear to be acting rudely toward you.

You may also concentrate on determining what your "anger triggers" are and doing all you can to get rid of them. For instance, if you notice that you get irritated and furious when you are forced to hurry, you should concentrate on creating more space in your schedule (even if it means saying "no" a bit more), and you should strive to remove the trigger that is causing you to feel this way. If there is a particular individual who causes you to feel agitated, you should make an effort to reduce the amount of influence that they have over your life if you find that communicating with them initially does not resolve the issue.

It is also essential to acquire the skill of learning how to let go of resentments and anger that is carried over from each day. If you can manage it, try not to face the morning still harboring resentment over the previous night's events. Put your focus on forgiving others, even if doing so requires you to cut someone out of your life who has harmed you in some way, so that you may go on with your life. This becomes much simpler to do when you focus your attention on the here and now as much as you possibly can.

Meditation and other activities that assist reduce stress might also make it easier to let go of resentment.1 Your primary focus should be on breaking free from whatever grip the past may still have on you. When you direct your focus on the here and now, it is much simpler to stop dwelling on the past and maintain a positive state of mind.

Help Others

It can seem intuitive that being a better person might be accomplished through assisting other people. We often consider "good people" to be individuals who are prepared to make sacrifices for the sake of others. According to the beliefs of a great number of people, this is what makes a person "good." On the other hand, because of the relationship that exists between altruism and psychological health, doing acts of kindness may also help us become better people.

The idea that "it's better to give than to receive" could really be true. It's possible that you're too stressed out and busy to provide assistance to other people when it's not really required, but cultivating your capacity to concentrate on the need of others may actually be quite beneficial to you as well. It's a well-known saying that helping others relieves stress, but it's also true that helping others is its own reward.

Helping others is beneficial to your mental health and may significantly increase the amount of tranquility you experience in your life.

Your efforts to be more altruistic will not only make the world a better place, but they will also make you a happier and more compassionate person. Because there are so many methods by which altruism may be expressed, this is a straightforward path to becoming a better person, and it is one that is open to all of us each and every day. This is really encouraging news indeed.

Utilize the Assets You Already Possess

The condition that psychologists refer to as "flow," in which a person loses track of time when engrossed in an emotionally satisfying activity or another activity that keeps them interested, is one that most of us are acquainted with. Flow is a mental state that may be achieved when a person is fully immersed in a pastime, when they are learning a new skill or topic, or when they are participating in activities that provide the perfect balance of ease and difficulty.

We experience stress whenever we feel like we have too much to do. If things are too simple for us, we could experience boredom; however, if we can find a happy medium between the two extremes, we can maintain a level of engagement that is highly beneficial.

Flow is a state that may be achieved by activities such as writing, dancing, producing, or learning new information that you can then pass on to others.

What may have been easy for you to do may have been difficult for others, and vice versa. Consider the circumstances in which you achieve this state the most often, and work to spend more time in those conditions.

The degree to which you feel immersed in an activity may serve as a useful indication of whether or not it is a suitable fit for you. When you're in the zone, you're able to make the most of your skills and abilities, which, as it turns out, is fantastic for both your mental health and your level of happiness. It is also a highly great thing for the rest of the world since your skills can typically be utilized to benefit others in some manner. This makes it a very positive thing overall.

You are well on your way to being a better person and a happy one as well when you learn enough about yourself to know what your finest abilities are and learn how to utilize them for the benefit of others.

Visualization: Use Your Imagination

Ask yourself this question: "If I had a magic wand, what would I like to see happen in the future of my life?" Visualize in great detail your perfect life and the things that should be a part of it, but don't worry about how you'll get there on the way there.

Spend a few minutes writing down or typing out on your computer a list of the alterations and objectives that would be included into this image. Be explicit in stating what it is that you desire. It is okay for you to want something that you do not seem to have any influence on, such as a partner who is tailor-made for you. Simply put it in writing.

You can decide to organize your life according to a one-year, five-year, and 10-year plan, similar to the way that many corporations do. (It does not have to be a plan that is fixed in stone; rather, it should be a list of desires and objectives.) Keeping in mind what you want to happen in the future may help you feel less trapped in the stressful aspects of your current life, and it can also help you recognize more choices for change when they come up in your life.

There are a number of approaches that may be taken to concentrate on transformation; however, the phases of change model has the potential to guide you to your best self more quickly and simply than a number of other routes. This paradigm of transformation is adaptable to any attitude you now hold and has the potential to work for the majority of individuals.

Be Self-Conscious

The process of becoming ready for a change is called preparation.

Taking concrete steps in the right direction to achieve the objective

Keeping up a new habit is what we refer to as maintenance.

In the event of a relapse, it is important to recommit yourself to achieving your objective and changing.

You shouldn't force yourself to make changes before you're ready, and you shouldn't give up if you find yourself backsliding; this is a forgivable and even anticipated part of the process of change. One of the most crucial aspects of this road to change is that you don't push yourself to make changes before you're ready. Having an understanding of this strategy for making changes will assist you in being a better person in any manner that you see fit.

To hear some advice on bringing about change, press play.

Take Care

It's possible that you won't always have a say in the events that occur in your life. You have some influence over how well you take care of yourself, which may have an effect on your stress levels and provide you the opportunity to develop as a person when you are forced to deal with the difficulties of life.

Taking care of oneself is absolutely necessary for developing resilience in the face of stresses that cannot be avoided. There are several reasons for this. If you are fatigued, not eating well, or just generally not feeling well, you will probably respond more strongly to the stress that you are now experiencing in your life. If you react negatively rather than responding from a position of calm inner power, you could even wind up causing additional issues for yourself.

On the other hand, if you do a good job of taking care of yourself (both your body and your mind), you'll be in a better position to deal with whatever comes your way, make the most of the resources you already have in your life, and really thrive rather than just survive as a result of the difficulties you encounter.

If you give your body, soul, and mind the attention they need, you can maintain yourself in the best possible form to deal with stress. That not only makes you more resilient to the difficulties in life that we all experience, but also to the difficulties in life that may be specific to you.4

Foundations of Good Self-Care

There are many other approaches to self-care that might be helpful, however the fundamental elements of self-care include the following components:

Sleep

Because a lack of sleep or sleep of poor quality may make you feel more stressed and impair your ability to come up with creative solutions to the challenges you encounter, getting enough of the right kind of sleep is critical to your mental and physical health. Your body will experience negative effects, both immediately and over the course of time, if you do not get enough sleep. A lack of quality sleep might also cause your weight to fluctuate.

Nutrition

The same may be said about a lack of proper nourishment. A bad diet may cause you to feel bloated and lethargic, in addition to causing you to gain more weight over time. You need the correct nutrition to meet the obstacles that life throws at you, yet when stress strikes, the food that we want the most is often bad food.

Relationships With Other People

Having a sense that you are linked to other people might make you feel more robust. When required, having supportive companions may assist you in processing unpleasant feelings, generating potential solutions, and taking your attention off of your difficulties. When we have a lot going on in our lives and a lot of stress, it may be difficult to find time to spend with our friends. However, the support and inspiration that we get from our friends often helps us become better people.

Downtime

Last but not least, it is essential to set aside some time for your own personal needs. This may take the shape of writing in a notebook or meditating, or it might be something as simple as going for a run or watching old episodes of a show on television at home. This is of utmost significance for introverts, although everyone needs time alone at least sometimes. Introverts are more in need of this.

Have Friendships

Our friendships have the potential to provide a safe refuge for us in times of hardship while also assisting us in growing as individuals. They may also be a big cause of stress when a disagreement is handled badly or when it is allowed to fester for an extended period of time. The wonderful thing about this is that putting in the effort to become a better friend, partner, and family member may also be a step toward being a better person overall. This is the beauty of it.

Gain New Skills

Gaining skills in dispute resolution may help you enhance your relationships as well as yourself. Techniques for anger control, being a good listener, and understanding the other side of a disagreement are some of the abilities that fall under this category.

Moral

These items have the potential to assist us in becoming better versions of ourselves. They have the ability to reduce the amount of stress we encounter in our relationships, so contributing to the improvement of such relationships. Close relationships often provide lots of opportunity to practice these abilities as you are working on developing them, which means that you might perhaps even learn to enjoy the opportunities when they present themselves and feel less irritated when they do.

Chapter Fifteen

Be Mentally Strong

Everyone has the goal of having a successful beginning to the year, but it's as crucial to have a successful ending. There are a lot of New Year's resolutions and objectives that never get accomplished because we get sidetracked by the events that are occurring in our lives, and also because we haven't built up the mental fortitude to keep going once the first burst of motivation from the New Year wears off.

Having a strong mental fortitude, on the other hand, is one of the most important factors in achieving one's objectives and succeeding beyond what was first envisioned. When you practice self-discipline, you strengthen your capacity to make excellent decisions that get you closer to achieving your goals. Keep in mind that you shouldn't give up on getting what you truly desire just so you may have some pleasure right now.

Being mentally tougher does not imply that it has to be a difficult or laborious process; the following advice and suggestions might be of assistance to you. If you want to be stronger mentally, just like you need to perform exercises to maintain your muscles strong if you want to be stronger physically, you need to undertake exercises to help create the habits and beliefs that will help you become stronger mentally.

Find routines and tiny suggestions throughout the day to keep your energy up, a positive mind-set, and help establish habits and skills that will help move you ahead and keep you feeling good about what you're doing. This is one of the greatest methods to build mental strength, and it's one of the best ways to grow mental strength overall. In the meanwhile, you are enhancing your mental power in a manner that will not leave you feeling weary or overwhelmed.

By putting a couple of these suggestions into practice, you may position yourself to have a psychologically healthier and happier year:

1. Put yourself to bed.

When you wake up and make your bed first thing in the morning, you're already ahead of the game in terms of productivity and having a good start to the day. Do you recall the proverb that said, "The condition of your bed is the condition of your head?" There is a great deal of validity to what you say. Although it can seem to be a little step, there are really quite a few advantages to doing it.

Those who routinely make their beds report feeling more satisfied with their life, are more productive, and have a greater sense of satisfaction and achievement in their day for all of the activities they do. Because of this one simple change, you'll develop the habit of completing assignments as soon as you can in the morning. What a wonderful sensation it is to have already accomplished one of your morning chores before you have even washed your teeth!

2. On a daily basis, compliment and encourage yourself.

Make a pact with yourself to reduce the amount of negative self-talk you have and increase the amount of positive things you say to yourself. It's possible that at first you'll feel stupid when you start acting as your own cheerleader in your thoughts, but just think about how amazing it'll feel as your life becomes better and better thanks to the choices you make. The choices you make today are what will keep you going in the direction of your goal.

A negative idea may creep its way into your head pretty fast; when you catch it, simply acknowledge that it's not true (even if you have to say it out loud) and replace it with a happy one. Being attentive is important since bad thoughts can come in so easily.

3. Record every day anything that went well in writing.

You may put the list in a shoe box, a jar, a diary, or any other container you choose, but be sure you jot down something positive about each day. Your life will become more grateful as a result of this.

You won't only be able to look back at the difficult times or tough patches that made you want to give up at the end of the year; instead, you'll be able to sit down and reflect on the great things that you've experienced and done during the course of the year.

4. Make a list of the good things that can come from every obstacle.

Perspective has a significant role in life. If you alter the way you look at things, you can change your life.

Build up your positive mental strength by writing down good elements and things you may be learning from the obstacles rather than complaining, getting angry, or disappointed (using in negative self-talk) about any issues that may come up in the future. This will help you avoid engaging in negative self-talk. Find something each day for which you may be thankful and make it a point to express that gratitude.

5. Make happy mindful practices part of your routine while commuting mindfulness refers to paying attention to the now moment by moment.

Practice being pleased in the present moment in order to acclimate yourself to contentment.

Take an experience, a moment, or a memory from a time when you felt good about yourself, and allow yourself to bask in that sensation. Look at how it sits in your body, how your thoughts change, how your body changes, and what it feels like; see if there are any colors that it may possibly feel like.

Get Your Hands on the Most Effective Productivity Tools

You are going to need some helpful toolkits if you want to be more organized, focused, and enthusiastic in order to achieve the goals that you have set for yourself.

Balance Your Life.

Spend some time with the joyful state you're in. At the conclusion of it all, pay attention to the sensation of pleasure and joy; these emotions originate inside you, and they appear on their own when you are present in the here and now with mindfulness.

6. Make a habit out of becoming your own best friend every day.

This is an excellent method for developing mental toughness since it teaches us to depend on ourselves and not to rely on the assistance of others when we are in need of support because we are able to provide it for ourselves.

The next time things doesn't go quite as planned, or you start to insult or criticize yourself, take a moment to stop and ask yourself:

Would I put up with it if my best friend treated me like this? or "Would I behave in this manner toward my closest friend?"

The answer to this question is probably not, and it is a fantastic idea to love yourself just as much, if not more, than you love your closest buddy.

7. Get in the habit of saying "No" without providing an explanation.

It's possible that somewhere down the line, as a culture, we made the decision that in order to say no to anything, we have to have a reason, and that the simple fact that we don't want to do it is not an acceptable justification. If you notice that you are thinking along such lines, then you should get rid of that line of thought.

Learn to say no. You are under no need to justify your choices or justify your conduct to anybody else about the reasons why you do not wish to do anything.

8. Dedicate at least twenty minutes of each day to acts of self-care.

No matter who you are or what you do, if you don't take some time to truly thoroughly care for yourself, you'll ultimately run out of love and compassion for the people around you, and then you won't be able to love and care for those around you. This is true regardless of what you do or who you are.

Self-care may be something as involved as getting a manicure or spending the day at a spa, or it can be as simple as shutting yourself in the bathroom for five minutes so you can have some quiet time to yourself. It doesn't matter what it is, but you should be sure to establish some space for yourself and/or activities that leave you feeling satisfied and content.

9. Dedicate at least some time each day to a pastime or activity that makes you happy.

This is an excellent method of taking care of oneself. Check to see if there isn't a pastime or action that you might take pleasure in only due to the fact that it improves your mood.

You'll find that the self-assurance and self-belief you get in one area of your life will transfer to other aspects of your life as you grow more skilled and competent in that area. You will get mentally stronger as you face the more challenging portions of your chosen objective if you have a happy attitude and find delight in the activities you like doing in your spare time.

10. Resolve to complain less and express gratitude more regularly as a goal for yourself.

Complaining not only makes you difficult to be around, but it may also have a significant negative impact on your mental health if you do it on a regular basis. Find something to be thankful for rather than simply always moaning about a predicament rather than making an effort to do so.

11. Commit yourself to getting a minimum of eight hours of sleep each night.

This is a massive deal! You've probably seen infants and young children going completely bonkers due to exhaustion. Adults are the same way, with the notable exception that we do not often find ourselves finally passed out in the midst of our dinner plate. When you are too exhausted, you are less able to think clearly, your mental strength decreases, your ability to think rationally is reduced to that of a child and your body reacts by producing more stress hormones.

This year, make getting enough sleep a top priority so that you can keep your mind healthy. If you are an athlete of any kind, you need to get at least eight hours of sleep every night; the more, the better. It is important to ensure that you give yourself enough time to rest and unwind before going to bed if you are experiencing high levels of stress. This will enable your body to get the most out of the time it spends sleeping.

12. Make it a priority to consume unprocessed food every day

Recent studies have shown a connection between your mental state and the health of your digestive tract, and one of the factors that has a direct bearing on your digestive tract health is the food that you put into your body.

You may alleviate some of the strain that is placed on your digestive system by lowering your consumption of foods that are known to cause inflammation. These foods include allergens, grains, dairy products, and alcohol. Less time spent unwell, increased levels of energy, and potential relief from the symptoms of sadness and anxiety are all benefits of having a digestive system that is in better condition.

Make an effort to shop solely on the perimeter of the grocery store, and consume only foods that you have prepared yourself. Read on for more information on healthy eating: What Is Clean Eating? (Important Advice & a Sample Meal Plan for Clean Eating)

13. Reduce the amount of time you spend on social media by half.

On social media, we have a tendency to present the best version of ourselves, which may lead to us attempting to compare our lives to the finest parts of another person's life. If you do this, you may end up feeling terrible and miserable about where you are in life and the wonderful things you've achieved as a result of your actions. It also has the potential to make you forget how many wonderful lives you impact throughout the day just by being the incredible person that you are.

Reduce the amount of time you spend on social media and use the extra time to spend reconnecting with people you care about, reading a book, or engaging in an activity you take pleasure in. Make sure that whatever you choose to do to pass the time is something that makes you feel better about yourself.

14. Post at least three inspiring quotes for daily reading and have them visible.

A few words of encouragement may go a long way toward keeping you on track when things become difficult and you get the impression that you are not making any headway.

Spend some time putting up a vision board or just hanging up a few motivational photographs or quotations in a place where you will see them often. When you're in a tough spot, hearing some kind words from others might go a long way toward helping you get through it.

Take a look at some of the wise words that have been spoken below: 50+ of the Most Inspirational Quotes Ever Said About Conquering Life's Obstacles

15. Spend ten minutes every day visualizing the accomplishment of your goals.

Spend some time visualizing not just the accomplishment of your objectives but also the difficulties you must face on the path to achieving them.

In addition to seeing yourself succeeding at your objective, you need also make an effort to properly plan out how you will get there. You may do this with the assistance of The Dreamers' Guide To Taking Action And Reaching Your Goal. It is a free handbook that may assist you in planning and organizing your day-to-day activities so that they are in line with your overall objective. Get your free copy of the guide here.

You should get in the habit of imagining how you will overcome prospective challenges. Imagine that you have already achieved all of your objectives and that you are basking in the glory of your success.

16. Free yourself from the obsession to please other people

Many times, in an attempt to be a nice person, we overextend ourselves and commit to activities that we really don't want to undertake. This may lead to burnout and stress.

Accept the idea that you won't be able to make everyone happy. Let go of the desire to prioritize the happiness and ambitions of others above what is best for you, both in terms of your health and your level of happiness.

17. Allocate a portion of your monthly income for a rewarding activity.

It doesn't even have to be a large event as long as it's something entertaining. It may be something you wouldn't ordinarily allow yourself to reach for, such as purchasing a new clothing, going to the movies, or getting yourself your favorite bubble bath – anything that will make you grin and feel fantastic when you come into touch with it.

Allow yourself to indulge in a little luxury once a month or once every few weeks. This might be doing something as simple as lighting a fresh candle or taking a relaxing bath with your favorite bubble bath product.

18. If you're involved in unhealthy relationships or activities that sap your vitality, cut them out of your life.

Move to a place that will celebrate you. Engage in activities that bring forth the childlike wonder in you. Build up your mental fortitude by surrounding yourself with supportive people and severing ties with those who bring you down.

It's not easy to cut ties with unhealthy people or environments, but in order to be stronger, you need to make a commitment to yourself. You'll have more energy and more enjoyment throughout the day if you eliminate the mental and emotional drain caused by the situation.

19. Eliminate the word "should" from your vocabulary as much as possible.

Consider the most recent instance in which you felt like you should be doing something. Wasn't exactly a notion that brought a smile to your face, was it?

The word "should" is often accompanied with thoughts of duty and significant responsibility, and very seldom by feelings of delight. The word "should" often brings with it feelings of harsh self-criticism and judgment, neither of which are helpful to the foundation you're working on constructing this year to become more psychologically resilient.

Instead of using the word "should" in your statement, try rephrasing it such that it focuses on something you are looking forward to accomplishing. As an example, you may say something like, "I would like to be mentally stronger." or "I would like to have a healthier physical appearance."

20. Keep a journal for a page or fifteen minutes, whichever comes first. Morning or evening, either way.

If you prefer to write in a diary first thing in the morning, consider writing about your dreams, dumping all of your worries or anxieties onto the paper, and using your writing as a creative outlet for anything that may have been keeping you up at night. It is also a terrific method to put down your objectives and inspirations for the day, to get a sense for what you want to see happen, and to formulate an action plan.

If you prefer to write in your diary at night, use this time to reflect on everything that may have caused you stress over the day and to give thanks for all you got right.

Remember the following no matter what strategy you choose to use this year:

Your mental muscles may be strengthened via constant, positive exercise, and over time, you will grow mentally stronger as a result of this!

Chapter Sixteen

We cling on to things for a number of reasons.

However, they may all be boiled down to a select few core feelings, including fear, wrath, and sorrow.

Fear of the unknown or the sensation that we are not in control of our circumstances often sets off these feelings in people.

We have a natural tendency to cling more desperately to the things we are familiar with if we feel as though we lack control or confidence in our lives.

There are occasions when this occurs regardless of whether or not the aforementioned items are beneficial or healthy.

Let's go a little more into these feelings and see how they can be influencing our capacity to let go of things:

The Impact Of Fear

We could be terrified of new things or of changing our current situation. It's possible that we're worried about giving up what we have. It's possible that we're terrified of being lonely or that we're not good enough. The fight-or-flight reaction may be triggered by fear, and this might cause us to cling to objects in an effort to protect ourselves from potential danger.

The Impact Of Anger

We could feel furious with the person we're with or the circumstances we're in right now. It's possible that we're frustrated with ourselves for being unable to let go of the past. When one is angry, it might be difficult to see things clearly and to make judgments that are objective. When we are overcome by feelings, we may behave rashly in an effort to recover control of ourselves.

We may feel melancholy over things that happened in the past or about the things we've lost. It's possible that the prospect of change or the unknown future makes us depressed. Feelings of helplessness and immobility are common outcomes of being sad. Apathy is an emotion that often shows itself as languid, lazy motions and a general disinterest in life. We do not have the necessary energy or the drive to let go of what we are clinging to.

The experience of any or all of these feelings is a normal and appropriate reaction to stressful circumstances. However, if we allow them to take control of our lives, they might prohibit us from living the lives we want to live.

It is essential that we acquire the skills necessary to control these feelings in order to be able to make rational choices on what is best for ourselves.

Why Let Go?

Despite the fact that letting go of things could make one feel anxious, experiencing the relief that comes after doing so can be quite empowering. It's possible that letting go of things may turn out to be the answer to the troubles you've been having all along.

When you free yourself from the pain and suffering that have been a part of your life, you'll find that a general release of pressure and tension is one of the many advantages that you'll be able to enjoy. Things will, in general, have the sensation of being unrestricted, open, and unhurried.

After you have learned to let go of something, you may find that your life has more room and you have more freedom in the following ways:

Reduced levels of stress and anxiety, which leads to improvements in both mental and physical health.

You will have more time and energy to devote to the activities and concerns that are most important to you.

Better understanding of what it is you want out of life and how to go about getting it

When you learn to communicate with others and with yourself more effectively, your relationships with both parties will improve.

As you let go of the past and move into the present, you will feel an overwhelming sensation of tranquility, peace, and pleasure.

You may find it difficult to let go of things in the beginning, but as you can see, the rewards are well worth the effort. You'll enjoy a high quality of life thanks to the various perks that come your way as a result. The question now is, how can you learn to let go of things?

The following eleven techniques may be helpful to you:

1. Acknowledge And Accept Your Emotions

It is essential to recognize how you are currently experiencing as well as the reasons behind why you are clinging to anything. Once you have gained an understanding of your feelings, you may start working through them.

There are instances when feelings such as rage are only a disguise for other, deeper emotions such as fear or grief. When you've identified the source of your emotions, you'll be in a better position to deal with them in a healthy way.

lady sitting calmly and observing the waves of the ocean letting things go in a relationship and how to do it

You may put how you're feeling and why you believe you're hanging on to anything down on paper. When you have a greater understanding of your feelings, you will be able to start working through them.

2. Make It A Habit To Take Slow, Deep Breaths

When we are desperately trying to hang on to something, one of the first things that happens is that we stop breathing. It causes us to keep tension in our muscles, which in turn contributes to feelings of worry and anxiety in our bodies.

You may help relax your body and mind and let go of the stress you're hanging on to by learning how to take deep breaths and practicing them regularly.

You may utilize this simple but powerful technique in whatever circumstance you find yourself in. Deep breathing. Just inhale deeply through your nose and focus on filling your lungs completely from the bottom to the top.

Then, carefully let all of the air out of your lungs by exhaling through your mouth. Repeat this a few times until you feel that both your body and your mind are beginning to relax.

3. Communicate With A Reliable Pal

When we are unable to move on and must continue to cling to something for an extended period of time, we may find that we get disoriented in our thoughts. This might make it challenging to have a clear perspective on the situation and to come to conclusions that are in our best interests.

If you want to get clarity and perspective on your current situation, talking to a reliable friend or member of your family may assist.

Your close buddy can provide you with the opportunity to talk out both your thoughts and emotions by acting as a sounding board for you. They could also be able to provide you with some useful advise or insights that you hadn't thought about previously, which is a possibility.

4. Speak With A Professional Counselor Or Psychotherapist

If you are having trouble letting go of anything on your own, speaking with a therapist or counselor about your situation may be of tremendous assistance. As you go through your feelings, they are able to provide you the support and assistance of a trained expert.

Therapists are educated to assist individuals in working through their emotions and are able to provide helpful tools and methods for letting go of the past.

If you need to learn how to let things go in a relationship, you may also get help from a therapist who specializes in couples counseling.

They can teach you and your spouse how to communicate more clearly and how to let go of the past in a way that is healthy for both of you.

You may do a search online for therapists in your area or contact your primary care physician for a recommendation if you are unclear how to get started.

5. Start A Gratitude Practice

One of the most effective strategies for letting go of negativity is to begin cultivating an attitude of appreciation. When you concentrate on the things for which you are grateful, it becomes far more difficult to harbor resentment, wrath, and other unfavorable feelings.

Keeping a thankfulness notebook is a great way to get started with a gratitude practice. Every day, take a few minutes to jot down three things for which you are thankful.

You may also cultivate an attitude of thankfulness by making it a daily effort to reflect on the people and experiences that bring you joy.

Put your attention on your heart, and just let a sense of thankfulness to flow over you. You could also find it helpful to express your gratitude aloud for the things that you have to be thankful for.

6. Treat Yourself To A Relaxing Massage Or Other Bodywork Treatment

Letting rid of tension and stress may be beneficially accomplished via the use of massage and other forms of bodywork.

When you get a massage, the muscles in your body release all of the stress that it has been keeping bottled up for so long. It has the potential to make you feel more at ease and relaxed as a result.

Freely embracing one another couple letting things go in a relationship and how to do it

Therapies that focus on the body, such as acupuncture, chiropractic care, and reiki, may also assist you in letting go. Because of these treatments, the energy in your body is brought into balance, and any blockages that may be causing you to hold onto stress are released.

Talking to a holistic health practitioner about your treatment options might be helpful if you are having trouble deciding which modality would work best for you.

7. Get Away For A While

The contexts in which we find ourselves may have a big influence on how we are feeling. When you are surrounded by constant reminders of what you are attempting to let go of, it may be challenging to move on to something new. Taking a vacation and getting away from everything is often the most effective method to let go of things.

Going on vacation may help you unwind and refresh your mind and body. It may also provide you with a new point of view and introduce you to new things, both of which may assist you in diverting your attention away from something that you are attempting to let go of.

Even if you are unable to take a full vacation, even just getting away for the weekend or spending a day in the great outdoors may be beneficial.

8. Embrace A Spiritual Practice

People are able to achieve a feeling of calm and a connection to something that is greater than themselves via the practice of spirituality. Taking up a spiritual practice might be of tremendous assistance to you if you're having trouble letting go of things in your life.

You will have a stronger sense of being supported and linked to something larger as a result of this, which will be beneficial to you when you are going through a difficult period.

You have a wide variety of options available to you in terms of spiritual activities to engage in. Praying or attending religious services may be quite comforting to some individuals.

Others discover that activities such as meditation, yoga, and treks in the wilderness enable them to sense a stronger connection to the environment around them.

To get the benefits of spirituality, it is not necessary to adhere to any one religion. Find a practice that enables you to feel more connected and at peace with yourself and the world around you. This is the most essential thing.

9. Start An Exercise Routine

The release of pent-up tension and emotions may be achieved to a great extent via physical activity. When you exercise, your body produces endorphins, which are chemicals that have the ability to lift your mood.

In addition, regular exercise may help you get a better night's sleep, which can be beneficial if you're having trouble letting go of something because you're feeling overwhelmed or nervous about it.

There are many other methods to be in shape than going to the gym, so don't feel like you have to force yourself to go. You may go for a run, enroll in a dancing class, or even simply do some exercises at home using your own bodyweight.

It is essential that you locate a pastime that you take pleasure in and this enables you to alleviate some of the stress that you are currently experiencing.

10. Meditate

Let go of whatever is holding you back and practice meditation instead. You let go of your ideas and concentrate on paying attention to your breathing instead. Just for a little while, you forget about everything that's going on in your life and allow yourself to just exist.

Meditation is a great tool to help you find peace and tranquility when you're going through a difficult time letting go of something. Additionally, it may assist increase your attention and concentration, which can be beneficial if you are experiencing feelings of being overwhelmed.

You may choose a practice of meditation that is suitable for you since there are many different methods to meditate. You might participate in a guided meditation session, practice mindfulness meditation, or just sit in quiet and concentrate on your breathing.

11. Donate Items To Those In Need

If you are the kind of person who has a hard time letting go of things, it may be beneficial to sell or donate some of the items you own. It's possible that giving stuff away can make you feel less burdened and more at peace.

Consider what you're clinging to and why you're doing so. You should make an effort to let go of anything that you are clinging to because it brings up memories of something or someone in your past.

Pay attention to the ways in which your products may significantly benefit other people. For instance, if you have a guitar laying around the house that you never use but you do have a friend who is interested in learning how to play, you should take pleasure in the fact that you can offer it to your buddy and help them on their path to becoming a better musician.

Giving away tangible objects can ultimately assist you in letting go of emotions, thoughts, and ideas that are no longer beneficial to you. This ethical act will make you joyful and pleased, and it will also help you let go of feelings and concepts that no longer serve you.

Survive

The act of clinging to something is a survival strategy. This is how we defend ourselves from being injured or experiencing pain. However, there are moments when the things we cling to are no longer doing us any good. Try one of these 11 techniques if you're having trouble letting go of something you care about.

It will become much simpler to let go of the things in your life that are no longer beneficial to you as you gain experience and time. This will allow you to create place in your life for the things that are beneficial.

What do you found to be useful when you are having trouble letting go of something?

Chapter Seventeen

Think about examining whether or not the discomfort is bearable.

When you've been injured for a long enough period of time, it's possible that you'll become accustomed to the emotional anguish. Perhaps you have a sense of comfort and recognition. It's possible that you've come to accept it as a fundamental aspect of who you are. Keeping your anger at that individual may make you feel more secure since it allows you to maintain your distance from them.

The discomfort of maturing may be quite genuine. It's possible that walking away from the things you've been thinking and feeling for a very long time can make you feel uneasy. On the other hand, it's possible that letting go may lead to healing, pleasure, and mental tranquility.

If you find yourself asking, "Why can't I let go?" then you could be one of the few people for whom this is true. These questions may assist you in beginning the process of letting go of the past:

Do you stand to gain anything additional if you continue to concentrate on the things that are causing you pain?

Do memories of the past prevent you from pursuing new relationships or participating in new experiences?

Do you avoid confronting the source of your emotional anguish since doing so would require you to resolve it?

What would your life be like if you stopped dwelling on the past and just moved on?

If you took on a different position in the circumstance, what do you think would happen?

RELEASE IT

Sometimes, in order to heal, you need to first allow yourself to experience it. It may be more detrimental to you in the long term and make it more difficult to let go if you bottle up your thoughts and feelings. This is especially true if you keep thinking about the past and the things that have wronged you.

Your mood, your relationships, and even your capacity to be productive and creative might be negatively impacted if you keep thinking the same negative ideas over and over again.

You should make an effort to discover healthy methods to communicate how you are feeling. Getting rid of the emotional energy might make it easier for you to cease ruminating.

Think about participating in activities that will allow you to vent your emotions in a protected environment. Take, for instance:

journaling with different prompts

You may choose whether or not to send the letter you write to the individual who wronged you.

expressing your suffering via play or art if you find it difficult to speak or write about it; finding a trustworthy friend, family, or therapist with whom you can talk about your experiences and how you're feeling;

Accept Responsiblity

When you take responsibility for your actions, it does not imply that you have to accept blame for things that have occurred to you in the past. Realizing how much of your energy you are devoting to remembering or experiencing things that are no longer part of your present is the first step in this process. It also involves making the conscious decision to direct your attention elsewhere.

When you refuse to let go of your sorrow, anger, or painful memories, you are forcing yourself to relive an unpleasant event over and over again. It's possible that this will prevent you from moving on from the past, which is now something you can no longer alter.

Accepting responsibility means you are also claiming your power and making the decision that you will not allow others to influence how you feel or how you conduct your life.

It's possible that you didn't have a choice in the matters that caused you pain in the past, but you have today. You have a choice today about where you will place your thoughts and feelings.

The perception that this is a challenging undertaking is normal and appropriate to have. Either the pain is so excruciating that you can't help but concentrate on it, or you have no choice but to deal with the repercussions of your actions. However, there is still hope for recovery.

If you're having trouble letting go of the past, you may want to talk to a mental health expert about how you can improve your coping skills and make it easier for yourself to move on. You deserve it.

Make An Effort

When you fixate on things that have happened in the past, you may not have much space in your heart and head for new experiences, especially ones that could offer you pleasure.

Your inability to let go of the past may increase the likelihood that you will overlook the positive aspects of your present.

Take into consideration the following actions to clear the way for the new and to let go of the old:

Establish personal as well as professional objectives for the near future.

Practice thankfulness in order to free your mind to concentrate on the excellent things happening right now.

Evaluate the quality of the connections you currently have and prioritize cultivating the ones that are beneficial to you.

Make it a monthly goal to try out a new pastime or activity, clean and arrange your surroundings so that you may donate or get rid of things that aren't serving you anymore, and create new friendships or work to enhance existing casual connections that have the potential to develop into lifelong companionships.

Learn how to bring your attention back to the present moment whenever your thoughts stray to the future or the past by engaging in one act of self-care per week and practicing mindfulness.

Participate in charitable endeavors that might potentially improve your mood by assisting other people in finding good leaders and mentors that are kind and empathic in their leadership.

Put Yourself First

Putting yourself first requires you to make deliberate choices in all aspects of your life. This might begin with the realization that selecting what is beneficial for oneself does not equate to acting in a self-centered manner.

Putting oneself first could entail regaining your power by concentrating on healing in the here and now rather than dwelling on what has caused you pain in the past. It's about coming to terms with the fact that you do matter.

Consider Getting Help

Try reaching to treatment to investigate how to let go of the past and harmed you've experienced setting boundaries with other individuals who may need to remember or examine the past when you're not ready to making life choices that make you are feeling secure, at peace, or upbeat, indeed on the off chance that others do not concur reframing considerations which will increment your uneasiness or pity to center on confident considerations locks in in self-compassion and self-respect

Putting yourself first could also mean looking into other avenues where you might find forgiveness.

Chapter Eighteen

FORGIVENESS

If someone has caused you pain and left you with a profound emotional wound, it is in your best interest to educate yourself on how to forgive them. In point of fact, the ability to forgive others is critical to one's health. It's been shown that unresolved sentiments of grief and hurt are at the basis of many mental health issues, notably depression, anxiety, and addiction. However, we have the ability to overcome these issues by engaging in the practice of forgiving others.

When you forgive someone, you release yourself from the role of victim and begin the process of moving on with your life. You will be liberated from the agony of those emotional scars, and you will be able to look straight forward to start a new chapter in your life. Instead of wasting your time hating, resenting, brooding, and questioning "Why did this happen to me?" you will do all of these things. You will be able to inquire as to "What's next?" in its place.

Forgiving

All of us, to a greater or lesser extent, are afflicted with what I refer to as a "love wound." The particulars of our unique traumas and the extent to which we were affected by them are the only things that set us apart from one another. Our feeling of goodness, our sense of connectivity to others, and our sense that we live in a safe and caring cosmos are all impacted when we suffer a love wound. Additionally, it does damage to our ability to love both ourselves and other people.

This love wound is the cause of a great deal of anguish and suffering, including depressed thinking, anxiety, loneliness, humiliation, rage, and addictive behaviors. Those who have suffered from this love wound have also experienced immense agony. It is only by healing these wounds that we will be able to alleviate the emotional pain we are experiencing and address the mental health disorders that have developed as a direct consequence of these sentiments. These feelings include intense feelings of isolation, rage, sadness, anxiety, and an overwhelming feeling of emptiness.

We may continue to "medicate" and cover up these sentiments with excessive drinking, recreational drugs, or habits such as gambling, out of hand shopping, excessive eating, or sexual interests that go beyond the pale if we don't forgive until we reach a point where we can let go of the past.

GET IN TOUCH WITH IT TO HEAL IT

Feel it in order to heal it. Pain is experienced by everyone, cannot be avoided, and, as we shall see, is sometimes even beneficial and essential. Think about it: the sensation of pleasure wouldn't exist if it weren't counterbalanced by the sense of suffering. As long as we are alive, we will continue to be a part of the global drama of opposites, which includes both pleasure and suffering.

If you don't allow yourself to experience the pain, you won't be able to find a solution to it. If you want to heal it, you have to let yourself feel it. There are methods to progressively give yourself up to your suffering without being overpowered by it. The willingness to do anything is essential. To alleviate your suffering will involve some work on your part, but be assured that the work will be amply rewarded! Try not to give up. It may take some time to undo the effects of the pain and devastation it has caused in our lives.

Anger is a severe kind of resentment that we might feel against other people or even toward ourselves. When we are able to provide grace to ourselves in the form of forgiveness—both of ourselves and of others—we are freed from these toxic sentiments.

The Art Of Dealing With Angry And Resentful Feelings

However, forgiveness is not something that can be done with a simple decision to do so. The cultivation of the circumstances essential for genuine forgiveness to take root is the source of true forgiveness. How can you grow your capacity for forgiveness? First, it's important to acknowledge that we've all suffered pain and contributed to the suffering of others. Because of our limited focus on ourselves or because of our ignorance, we inflict pain not only on other people but also on ourselves, and everyone suffers with this aspect of the human condition.

Take a moment to reflect on the expense that harboring resentments might incur. What kind of impact do they have on your disposition and perspective? Consider the repercussions of giving in to the temptation to harbor self-righteous grudges, and take note of how your hostility and resentment snuff out your pleasure. Having this information in front of you will assist in easing the hold that those grudges have on you. Investigate the circumstances and factors that may have contributed to the harmful behavior of either you or the offender. Your comprehension will inspire compassion and forgiveness for all of our affliction and ignorance, and we will be grateful.

Imagine the individual who caused you pain when you were a little kid. Remember that everyone of us was once naive, and that none of us had a say in the genes we inherited, the parents we were raised by, or the environments in which we grew up. Recognize the ways in which these circumstances influence our behavior, as well as the behavior of others. It is possible that initially it may be simpler to forgive the youngster than it will be to forgive the adult. Recognize that we may forgive ourselves as well as other people for our lack of awareness in the past, given that awareness is a quality that can be developed through experience and inquiry.

Having unreasonable expectations might lead to feelings of resentment. When we have an expectation that Reality would be something other than what it is, we experience feelings of bitterness. To be able to let go of resentment, we have to let go of the urge to be flawless and the need to have things happen precisely as we want it to.

11 STEPS

Here are 11 steps to forgive someone.

One way to think about forgiveness is as a process that takes place over time and involves a number of phases. You'll breeze through some of them, while others will take much more time. It is a really personal and unique experience. If you discover that you have previously completed any of these actions while reading this, there is no need to carry out those activities again at this time. Simply go to the next step. If required, return to the stages that came before.

1. Grieve

It is only through our own suffering that we may find the way to forgiveness. In order to forgive someone, you need to first go through the process of mourning the losses, disappointments, and traumas you've experienced. First and foremost, you have to admit the wrongdoing that was committed against you. Feelings such as pain, betrayal, fury, revenge, guilt, humiliation, and fear are included in this category.

Recognize and accept the depth of your suffering. The next step is to work through the pain and put it into proper perspective. The act of opening up about the wrongs done to you to a select few individuals in your life in whom you have complete faith is an essential component of the healing process. When you find yourself in a bind, ask for assistance.

You will ultimately be able to let go of your anger, shame, guilt, and blame for the offender's acts as part of your processing and healing from the trauma. Your suffering will gradually lessen as the mourning process progresses. Keep in mind, however, that in order to go through this process successfully, you may need the assistance of a therapist.

2. Give Yourself Some Time To Consider The Advantages Of Forgiving Someone As Opposed To Harboring Resentment Against Them

Pay attention to the ways in which holding grudges has harmed you and contaminated your life. When you see how your grudges are hurting you and make the decision

to forgive for the benefit of yourself, the bitterness you feel
will begin to subside.

3. Give Due Consideration To Your Feelings

Ignoring your suffering is the surest way to prevent you
from ever really forgiving yourself. Keep in mind that you
cannot forgive people until you have dealt with your own
anger, grief, and pain. If you have caused harm to other
people, there is no way to forgive yourself without first
working through the anguish of regret.

4. Stop Blaming

Do not put the responsibility for your life, your emotions,
your actions, or your well-being on anybody else. If you
continue down this path, you will spend the rest of your life
feeling like a victim. Accept the whole and complete
responsibility for your life, including your happiness, your
attitude, and the things you do. Additionally, accept
responsibility for the way in which you react to everything
that occurs in your life. Maintain a balance between
aggression on one extreme and passivity on the other, and
practice assertiveness that is both polite and forceful. Your
objective is to safeguard oneself from suffering any
additional injury.

5. Make Mental Health A Priority

Observe that none of us are immune to the struggles of hostility, self-clinging, self-preoccupation, or selfishness. We inflict grief and suffering on one another either out of ignorance or because of our own anguish, and we all have gaps in our ability to love.

6. Make An Effort To Be Humble

Let go of the urge to constantly have things go your way in life and the drive to be flawless. Remind yourself that life is not only about you, but about all life, including other lives.

7. Let Go Of Expectations To Impossible To Fufill

When we have an expectation that reality (people, places, things, or events) would be different from what it really is, we experience resentment. Instead, you should anticipate everything to remain in its current state.

Eight Always Remember Your Morals

Simply because they are alive, every single person should be treated with the highest attention and respect at all times. This is because they are sacrosanct. Your unwavering regard encompasses not just those who have wronged you but also you yourself, and it extends even to those who have wounded you.

Consider judgment for what it really is: a fabrication that we superimpose on reality in order to judge its alleged "goodness" or "badness." Free yourself and others from the burden of judgment, and acknowledge that it is simply not your position to pass judgment on either yourself or anybody else. Because of this, you will be able to love and accept yourself and others for who you and they really are: human beings who are perfect in their imperfections.

9. Send Your Offenders Best Wishes For Their Future

When you really want the best for other people, it's difficult to hold grudges against them. The advantages of this exercise will offer you more inner peace over time as you continue to engage in it.

10. Be Merciful To Yourself

You may grow self-forgiveness in the same way that you cultivate forgiveness for others by using all of these same methods to yourself in the same way. Remember that you share humanity with other people, and have compassion for yourself, as well as for others. You are not any different from everyone else, and you do not deserve forgiveness any less than they do.

11. Get On With It

There is hardly much use in dwelling on the ways in which we have harmed other people or have been victims ourselves. Spending time reliving traumatic events from the past is, in the long run, a certain method to prevent oneself from moving on with one's life.

You have a choice: you may allow yourself to be a victim, harbor hatred against people who caused you damage, and spend your time wondering "why did this happen to me?" You may also ask yourself, "What should I do now?" You may free yourself from the role of victim by deciding not to make anybody else accountable for your health and happiness.

Take what you can from it, and then put it behind you. It is no longer a possibility; all that is left is the instant we are in right now.

Obtaining Peace By Giving Control To God

Forgiveness is crucial if you want to improve your mental health and overcome addiction, anxiety, or despair. It may also help you feel better about yourself. When making the choice to forgive, it is common to have to let go of feelings of intense fury and resentment directed against another individual, group of individuals, or even events or circumstances, such as a disease that has wreaked havoc on your life or the life of someone you care about. Almost usually, the first step in forgiving someone else is letting go of whatever resentment, blame, or shame you feel about yourself.

Everyone is motivated by their own self-interest. As you develop your awareness and become more "awakened," you will be able to feel that caring for yourself and caring for other people are two sides of the same coin. Your ability to judge others will diminish, and you'll be better able to forgive them if you look at things from a "unicentric" (concerned with everyone) point of view rather than a "egocentric" (just concerned with oneself) point of view. You'll also have the capacity to forgive people who haven't yet come to this realization.

In order for us to recover, we feel it is necessary to first accept our injuries and then work through the suffering. Changing our perspective on what took place might make it easier for us to handle the pain without being overwhelmed, despondent, or imprisoned by it or any addiction that may have resulted from it. If you have experienced major trauma in the past, working through this process with the assistance of a qualified trauma therapist (for referrals, see the list of resources below) may be beneficial to you.

The capacity for forgiveness is a personal strength that contributes to one's physical and mental well-being throughout the healing process. According to the findings of several academic research, practicing forgiveness—both toward oneself and toward others—can bring about feelings of contentment, mental calm, and a much-needed sense of life fulfillment and relief.

There are no potential drawbacks.

Chapter Nineteen

Have you ever pondered the reasons behind why individuals choose the paths that they do? What qualities distinguish a bad person from a good one? Should we make an effort to be decent, and if so, why is it important?

If you asked twenty individuals what it takes to be a nice person, you would probably hear twenty different replies. This is just a statistical probability. The qualities of character that different people think are admirable are determined by a number of different variables. One's religion, ethnic heritage, and the dynamics of their family all play a role in the formation of their own ideas and often affect how they perceive the world and the people in it.

In general, the majority of individuals have the aspiration to live a moral life. However, this objective cannot be accomplished if one does not first understand what characteristics constitute a "good" person. Many people experience tremendous anxiety or sadness as a result of the conflict they feel between wanting to be a nice person and possessing undesirable personality qualities. Later on in this piece, we will go through some of these problems and the solutions to them that we have found.

What Does It Mean to Be Good?

A great definition of the word "good" describes it as "virtuous, right, and commendable; kind, and benevolent."

Goodness is the only investment that never fails.

Qualities that define a morally upstanding person

A decent person often have habits or qualities that set them apart from others in noticeable ways. Some instances include the following:

Empathy

The meaning of the term empathy The capacity to empathize with another person's experiences and comprehend their emotional state by placing oneself in their shoes is the foundation of psychological study. Someone who is empathic communicates an awareness of how other people are feeling.

It is not only a vocal assertion of comprehension; rather, it is communicated as an emotional condition. When someone is suffering, their most common want is to have someone who can relate to what they are going through there with them.

Being a good person does matter.

Participate in self-improvement sessions with a licensed online therapist.

Honesty

Anyone who aspires to live a successful life should make it a priority to be honest, both with themselves and with other people. Being dishonest is a certain way to destroy a relationship, not to mention the impression you leave with other people.

Humility

To be modest is not the same thing as putting oneself through an embarrassing situation. Instead, a person who cultivates humility is one who is prepared to be good to others even when they do not anticipate receiving any benefit in return. A modest person is someone who is prepared to give of oneself and does not expect anything in return for their generosity.

Fairness

Being able to express an opinion without of prejudice requires a person to be free from the personal prejudices that cloud their judgment. Rather than being loyal to the views of other people, it demonstrates a dedication to the fundamental ideas of what is good.

Responsibility

Having the maturity to acknowledge and accept responsibility for one's own deeds is a symptom of a person who is morally upstanding.

Why It Is Important To Be A Good Person?

Your reputation will be shaped in part by your activities and behaviors. There are certain persons who have a reputation for being greedy, self-centered, or dangerous. Some people are seen to be kind, generous, and loyal companions. The possibilities that present themselves to you in life will be influenced, in addition to other things, by your reputation.

As was just discussed, the decisions we make in life have a tendency of following us for years, and sometimes even for the rest of our lives. In the following paragraphs, we will talk about the ways in which the decisions we make and our reputations impact our lives, as well as why it is important to be a decent person.

How Your Character Can Benefit (Or Hurt) Your Professional Life

Imagine for a second that you are the proprietor of a business and that you have an opening for a new member of staff. Two of the prospective prospects had quite impressive credentials. If you delve beyond the words on the candidate's résumé and contact references, you will find that one of the applicants is talked about in extremely favorable terms. You have been informed that she is highly accountable, honest, and has a lot of love for the job that she does. On the other hand, the references provided for the other applicant are not quite as glowing. You have been informed that he was discovered being dishonest in a few business agreements, that he was always late for work, and that he was unable to receive instructions or advise from superiors without being irritated. The experience that is detailed on those resumes doesn't appear to have as much weight all of a sudden, does it?

Developing habits of honesty and integrity is one approach to demonstrate to others that you are a "good person." If you go in a different direction, it can have a detrimental effect on your professional life.

The Positives, The Negatives, And Your Relationships

There is no question that our actions, whether positive or negative, will have an effect on the connections we have with other people. People will begin to question our sincerity and trustworthiness if we engage in negative behaviors and practices such as harmful habits or terrible behavior. On the other side, when individuals are looking to create a long-term friendship or an intimate connection, they look for people who have a giving attitude, who are honest, and who put others before themselves. It's about having a sense of security. Relationships are an investment, and those who want to have healthy relationships will look for people who make them feel comfortable rather than those who make them feel uneasy or cause them to doubt their own value.

The choice to behave morally is an internal one. No matter how much we learn about the positive and bad impacts our conduct has on ourselves and others, no one can compel another to be a really decent person. This is true regardless of the level of knowledge we obtain on the topic. Think about the advantages of being a decent person and the ways in which your actions may affect the course of your life for many years to come.

Having earned the respect of others, we are in a position to more readily take advantage of opportunities when they present themselves. Your current or future employers, along with your coworkers and peers, would think highly of you if they hear that you have the reputation of being a decent person. When other people respect you, you increase the likelihood that you will be able to have a beneficial effect on the lives of those other individuals.

Respecting Yourself If you have a hard time respecting yourself, it's likely that other people won't regard you very much either. Your feeling of pride and the right to respect yourself and your efforts will increase if you conduct yourself in a proper way, maintain honest routines, and have a strong work ethic.

A Sense Of Purpose Being Created By Our acts The results of our acts may either leave us with a sense of success or a feeling of regret. The development of a sense of purpose via the study and continual application of positive behavior. When we have a sense of direction and purpose in our life, we are more driven to take action and make positive changes.

When Being Good Seems Hard To Do

Have you ever had the feeling that no matter how hard you work, your life just doesn't seem to want to go in the direction that you want it to go? We all have days that seem to be a bit more challenging than others, and this is true regardless of the kind of history a person has. The adventure that is life. Every day ought to be lived for a specific reason. Even the ones that are awful.

The fight to be a decent person or to alter bad behaviors is a very real one for a lot of different people. You could acquire a better understanding of how your actions have impacted others by having a conversation with a close friend or member of your immediate family. Additionally, if the problem of being a good person is something that you struggle with but want to accomplish, getting the guidance of a counselor or therapist is an excellent method to share your emotions and discover ways to apply good practices. This is especially helpful if the issue of being a good person is something that you struggle with but want to achieve.

Chapter Twenty

In today's world, there is a lot that might cause worry for people, including divorce, job loss, and the possibility of terrorist attacks. And quite often, the cause is something that we have no control over. When is the right moment to seek professional assistance in order to learn how to better manage your anxiety?

Anxiety In Its Healthy And Unhealthy Forms

The "fight or flight" reaction is what causes anxious people to break out in a cold sweat, and according to Andrews, this response is what kept our early ancestors safe from grizzly bears and other frightening characters. "That rush of adrenaline is still beneficial to us in some situations," the author writes. Anxiety is a normal response to the very real pressures that people are under.

In the environment we live in today, "that reaction helps motivate us, prepares us for things we have to face, and sometimes gives us the energy to take action when we need to," explains Ross.

You have a significant job interview coming up, and the prospect has you in knots. So, as a result, "you spend a little more time getting dressed or rehearsing what you're going to say,". You have an appointment with the divorce lawyer, so you do some further reading and preparation. This type of worry might serve as a spur to perform to your full potential. It is helpful in providing protection for you."

To put people into an anxious state, however, it is not always necessary for there to be an actual danger; rather, it is sufficient for there to be the prospect of a crisis. "The challenge is to learn to temper that instinctive reaction by asking yourself, 'How significant is the risk?'" How probable is it that the danger will materialize?'".

The thing about anxiety is that it can take on a life of its own.Everything takes on the potential to become a catastrophe. The impossible has really come to pass. Therefore, there is always the potential for another catastrophe just around the bend.

The Price Paid In Anxiety

Your body will let you know when anxiety is having a negative impact on you. You are having problems falling asleep, eating, and focusing on tasks. You are experiencing headaches, and your stomach is giving you trouble. It's possible that you may even experience a panic attack, complete with a racing heart and a sense of dizziness.

The symptoms of anxiety may be quite similar to those of depression. Ross thinks that there is an occasional crossover between the two.

When anxiety gets so overpowering that it interferes with day-to-day activities -- when it stops you from going places, and when it prevents you from accomplishing things you need to do -- that is when you need treatment, according to Ross.

Generalized anxiety disorder is a more extensive condition that functions "like a worry machine in your head." "If it's not one thing, it's another," is a common expression. You've gotten to the point where you're putting things off to the point where you're almost frightened to take action. You put off coming to your child's school to speak to the teacher because you are overcome with anxiety over the situation, and as a result, you miss the appointment.

When individuals are experiencing such intense worry, "people are not making good decisions," according to Ross. They are either avoiding situations or are unable to rise to the challenge because the amount of anxiety they are experiencing is too great. They are unable to concentrate and keep their attention on the task at hand, which is why they procrastinate. It is having a significant impact on their day-to-day activities and routines. They may then be suffering from a more severe kind of anxiety and need the assistance of a trained specialist.

How Do You Deal With It?

"Get real," as the expression goes, is one strategy for coping with everyday worry. "Separate out the real risks and dangers that a situation presents from those that your imagination is making worse," is some advice that Ross offers. A new spin on an old saying, this one goes like this: "Take control of the things you can, and accept those you can't change."

"Ask yourself: What aspects of the circumstance are under your control? Where do you think you might improve things? Then carry out the necessary steps," is what she advises. "What are some things that you just have to learn to accept?" That is of utmost significance.

It is quite common to be able to break out of an anxiety cycle with the assistance of friends or family members -- someone who is able to assist you in working through your issues. When anxiety reaches this point, though, it is necessary to seek the help of a therapist, and possibly even medicine.

The following are two methods that therapists use in order to assist their patients in overcoming their anxiety:

Confronting Negative Ideas Is Important

Ask yourself, "Is this a thought that will lead to something positive?" Is it bringing me closer to the achievement of my objective? If it's merely an old, unfavorable notion that keeps popping into your head, then you need to be able to tell that thinking, "Stop." "That's difficult to do, but it's very important," Ross adds. "It's not easy."

Another message you might send to yourself is this one: Instead of letting your fear cause you to become immobile, try this instead: It's possible that I'll have to accept a job that I don't like as much, or that I'll have to travel farther than I'd want, but I'll do what I have to do now. At the very least, I will not have to worry about my money in the near future. After that, I'll be able to seek for something more suitable afterwards."

"to realize when you've done everything you can, that you need to move forward," Ross adds, is the most crucial thing.

Learn How To Calm Down

You could even need "breathing retraining," as Ross points out further. People have a habit of not breathing properly when they are nervous. People learn a certain kind of breathing called diaphragmatic breathing, which helps to relax the whole body. Try out some yoga, some meditation, or just go for a run. Exercising is a fantastic way to relieve stress and anxiety.

The most important thing you can do is to avoid making your difficulties worse. "There is a valid reason to feel bad when things are bad," she adds. "When things are bad, there is a legitimate reason to feel bad." "But if you don't deal with it, you're going to lose more than just a job. You're going to lose relationships, you're going to lose your self-confidence, and if you don't keep up with your profession, you may even lose technical ability. Make an effort to avoid adding to an already existing source of stress.

Your capacity to overcome worry and move on from it may often be affected by the kind of the adversity you have been forced to confront. "The more severe it was and the more surprising it was, the longer it is going to take to get over it," says Andrews. "The more surprising it was, the longer it was going to take." "It's possible that you'll be on cruise control for the next several weeks. Being sad might make situations more difficult to deal with. If you and your spouse decide to divorce, it might take anything from a few months to many years until you feel like your true self again.

But don't lose hope. "If you're doing well in one aspect of your life -- whether it's in your work or your relationships -- you're probably on the way," she adds. "If you're doing well in both, you're probably doing pretty good." "Fear and anxiety do not have the upper hand in your life anymore."

Medication For Disorders Related To Anxiety

An anxiety problem can not be cured by medication, but it may help keep it under control and function more normally. There are many choices available to choose from in the event that one's anxiety becomes severe enough to necessitate medical treatment.

Antidepressants, and notably SSRIs, have shown promise as a potential treatment for a variety of different anxiety disorders.

Benzodiazepines are another therapy option. These include drugs like Valium, Ativan, and Xanax. Benzodiazepines may be used alone or in conjunction with SSRI medicine. Because of the possibility of developing an addiction to these substances, it is not recommended to take them for an extended period of time. Other potential negative effects include feeling sleepy and irritable, as well as having trouble concentrating.

Beta-blockers have been shown to be effective in treating the physical manifestations of some types of anxiety disorders, most notably social phobia.

Chapter Twenty One

What does it take to be a decent person, and how might one go about becoming one?

The roadway is being traversed by two individuals, one of them is a retired fireman and the other is an elderly person using a cane. They were startled to see a home on flames as they came across it. Someone may be seen sticking their head out of a window on the second level and yelling, "Help me!" Help me!"

The majority of us do not often come into contact with properties that are currently on fire. However, we are faced with other sorts of moral judgments, such as whether or not we should try to get our nine-year-old grandson in for free at the zoo by pretending he is under the age of eight. Should we inform our brother-in-law if we find out that our sister is having an affair? According to Bloomfield, finding out how to be a decent person involves planning out how you will react to different situations.

Being excellent is not an end in and of itself; it's just a means.

Being excellent is not, in and of itself, sufficient justification for Bloomfield's pursuit of a goal. According to him, the ancient Greeks were the first to propose the idea of eudaimonia, which might be translated as a life blooming to its full potential. According to this theory, the only way to ensure that one's life is filled with joy and contentment is to live a good life. According to him, if we want to have the most fulfilling life possible, goodness is an essential quality to cultivate.

If you want to achieve that objective, there are certain straightforward tactics that may assist shed light on the way to get there.

Being a nice person and having happiness are inextricably linked to one another. You may discover your happy spot now with the aid of these simple suggestions for self-care.

Good People Have Morals

Understanding what drives people is an essential part of developing one's moral character.

It is essential to have an understanding of the reasons behind the actions that we do, in particular if there is a pattern of behavior that we would want to alter.

Children who are more empathic are more prone to utter prosocial falsehoods, which spare someone's emotions or smooth up social interaction. Young people who are more sympathetic are more inclined to tell lies. It is not as black-and-white as people often make it out to be; in fact, lying to someone else might be a means to show that you care about them.

In a similar vein, it is essential to have an understanding of the motivations that lie behind our "bad" behaviors when they are carried out in an antisocial manner. We might do something 'bad, like lashing out in anger or turning to drugs or alcohol, However, she explains that same activities could serve a greater cause.

Aperson who lacks the ability to regulate their impulses may not have been given the opportunity they need as a kid to articulate their needs; a person who numbs themselves with drugs or alcohol may be trying to avoid facing an unpleasant reality.

Everyone is naturally good. Developing self-compassion for behaviors that on the surface seem to be "bad" is the first step toward healing; after we have integrated these characteristics into our knowledge of who we are, we can begin to work toward letting go of them.

When we investigate "bad" ideas or behaviors, it may sometimes throw off our sense of who we are. After experiencing a blow to your confidence, the following are some strategies that might help you improve your self-esteem.

Do everything you can to help cure the planet.

In Judaism, we're largely defined by our actions." It's impossible to be a nice person while sitting on the sidelines. This idea is connected to the ancient Jewish philosophy known as tikkun olam, which may be translated as "to repair the world." According to her, our responsibility as human beings is to "fix what's been broken." It is our responsibility to not just look out for one another and ourselves, but also to work toward making the world we live in a better one.

According to this school of thought, goodness may be conceptualized as something that is founded on service.

The question "What good do I do in the world?" is perhaps a better one to ask oneself than "Am I a good person?".

Are you looking for some motivation? Examine the following examples of positive news reports from all across the globe.

Think about what people will say about you when they attend your funeral.

This difference may assist lead our own efforts to be more virtuous, which is especially helpful when we are feeling burdened or busy. Are we working for the things that we think are valuable and important? If not, what modifications are there that we can do to our lives to guarantee that we are living lives that we feel good about?

The following are seven words or phrases that should never be said during a funeral.

Fixing one's errors is an essential part of learning how to be a decent person.

Sometimes doing good must begin with admitting, accepting, and taking responsibility for our prior errors in order for us to go on and attempt to do better. This is because acknowledging, accepting, and taking responsibility for our mistakes allows us to move forward.

Judaism has very defined steps written out for things like repentance, You should begin by admitting that you have behaved inappropriately in some way. You owe it to the person you've wronged to make apologies to them. And remember to adjust your behavior accordingly the next time you find yourself in the same predicament.

Being a virtuous person does not imply that you never make a mistake; rather, it means that you figure out the best way to react when you do make a mistake. The capacity for goodness is not a set quality that is passed down from generation to generation; rather, it is something that may be evaluated, reevaluated, and developed through time. And coming to terms with the fact that making mistakes is an inherent part of being human might very well be one of the most useful tools we have for developing into better people.

Chapter Twenty Two

There are moments when we get the feeling that we are able to deal with everything that life may throw at us. There are also times when even the most little of setbacks might seem like an insurmountable obstacle. What exactly is the differentiating factor?

It's not the conditions that we find ourselves in at all. A good number of us are familiar with the feeling of being frustrated by something that, under normal circumstances, wouldn't get on our nerves. Then, we frequently have the ability to flip around and write off significant failures as just being a normal part of life.

The difference is not in what is occurring; rather, it is in the mental power that we possess. We are able to avoid getting sidetracked by negative ideas as a result of the mental power we possess. It assists us in getting back into the swing of things with the daily highs and lows of life. And, just like physical strength, it's a type of mental muscle that can be developed to increase general well-being; just like physical strength, it's something we can work on.

What exactly does "mental strength" mean?

To be mentally strong does not imply that one is never emotional, never complains, and never has any doubts. And the two do not always go hand in hand with mental disease. In point of fact, many individuals who struggle with disorders such as ADHD, depression, and other mental health issues are tremendously mentally strong. This is because they have had to put in a lot of effort to build coping methods.

In place of a singular, unchanging conception of what it means to be mentally fit, the concept of mental strength examines the following questions: How do you react when confronted with unpleasant feelings or challenges? Do you immediately begin to come up with answers, complain about how unlucky you are, or just try to let things pass you by?

What exactly does "mental strength" mean?

The cognitive and emotional talent of being able to reframe negative ideas and bad events is an essential component of mental strength. Being mentally strong, also known as having mental toughness, enables us to better withstand both the internal and external pressures that might undermine our sense of well-being and self-confidence.

When attempting to comprehend mental toughness, we might make advantage of the metaphor of bodily wellness. In the same way that physical strength is a part of being physically fit, mental strength is also a part of being mentally healthy.

Maintaining and enhancing your mental health may be accomplished via a comprehensive set of activities known as "mental fitness." Being mentally strong enables you to maintain your concentration in challenging situations, such as when an athlete must shout above the cheers of the crowd in order to score the game-winning goal. Although mental toughness might help you perform better under pressure, it is not always possible to maintain that level of performance over time. This type of severe strain may affect mental health even in athletes competing at the Olympic level.

On the other side, mental fortitude acts as a counterweight to extremes. Our capacity to perform successfully and sustainably in the face of obstacles and stress — without compromising our own health, sense of self, or mental well-being — is what we mean when we talk about resiliency. It is directly connected to the concept of resilience. In point of fact, athletes who earn an Olympic silver medal are often more resilient than those who win an Olympic gold medal.

To recap, mental toughness, mental fortitude, and mental strength are all aspects that contribute to mental fitness. The ability to shut out distractions and negative self-talk is a benefit of mental toughness. You may speed up your road to recovery by developing your resilience. Mental toughness enables us to keep going, and mental fitness is built up via all of these different kinds of training.

A fresh rallying cry for action.

What does it look like when mental power is put into action?

You can hardly contain your excitement over the upcoming presentation you'll be presenting to the higher-ups at your organization. While you are practicing your slides, a buddy of yours points out a weakness in the approach you are taking. Despite the fact that you have spent the last several weeks putting in a lot of effort to be ready for this, you are utterly caught off guard. Do you have time to completely consider the presentation that you are about to give?

When you consider what anxiety is and why it occurs in the first place, you'll see that those unpleasant feelings do serve a function. Anxiety serves the purpose of drawing our attention to prospective dangers so that we may devise strategies to deal with them. But it stops being adaptive and starts being harmful when the sensations of dread are so overwhelming that we can't move.

We are better able to fight off paralysis and fight back against the powers of dread and worry when we have mental strength. We are more able to reframe the anxiety and hear what it is trying to tell us when we have built up our mental power and are better equipped to do so. What kind of outcomes do we need to give some consideration to? What is the absolute worst thing that might happen? How can we best prepare for it in order to increase our chances of being successful?

The power of our minds has enormous repercussions for us in other areas as well. Developing your mental toughness has the following five benefits:

1. Less Stress

When you have a healthy mental state, you are better able to deal with the highs and lows, big and little, that life throws at you. You look at challenges as chances to learn and improve yourself. You are able to shift your perspective and have faith that you will prevail despite the magnitude of the challenges you face. After all, you've triumphed through significant challenges in the past.

One of the most effective methods to enhance your health and well-being is to learn how to better manage your stress. Reduced levels of stress are linked to a reduced likelihood of developing depression, anxiety, and a number of physical health issues.

2. Motivation

We lose both energy and motivation when our mental power is lacking. We get the impression that no matter what we put our minds to, undesirable outcomes will follow, and our efforts will be fruitless.

On the other side, those who have a high mental strength often have a high internal locus of control. This indicates that they consider themselves to be in command of the situations they find themselves in. That feeling of being in control is what drives people to keep trying, to improve, and to keep exploring for answers. People that are resilient are less likely to give up quickly.

To avoid putting things off till later, mental toughness carries with it the discipline and internal drive that are necessary. Those with a strong mental fortitude find it much simpler to launch themselves into new endeavors and see them through to their completion.

3. Exercise Discretion

Understanding what to listen to and more importantly, what not to listen to, is an essential component of being successful in life. Both the criticism we give ourselves and the criticism we get from others may easily throw us off. When you cultivate mental toughness, it becomes much easier to maintain concentration, even in situations in which other people disagree with you or in which you feel terrified.

Developing self-awareness and, as a result, the ability to regulate one's emotions requires a significant amount of discretion. You'll have a higher tolerance for unpleasant feelings as you acquire the ability to acknowledge and acknowledge yourself while experiencing them. You'll get an understanding, with the passage of time, of which feelings are worthwhile to pay attention to and which ones you should simply let go of.

4. Courage

When we have a strong sense of mental fortitude, we have less fear of making mistakes. It is far simpler for us to change into problem-solving mode, regardless of whether or not we are anxious about the possible consequence. Because we have a higher level of self-belief, we have a greater sense of confidence in our capacity to discover answers. Even more crucially, we are certain that we will be able to live through the most worst-case situation (if it ever occurs).

5. Adaptability

Increasing our propensity to seek out and implement ideas makes us more nimble and flexible. We spend less time ruminating on the things that aren't going as planned and more time concentrating on the ways in which we might attain the intended result. We are also willing to consider the possibility that success might be indicated by more than one method, solution, or outcome. Because we are not frightened of change, we do not get tied to the idea that everything should proceed precisely the way we want it to.

Chapter Twenty Three

Both physical exercise and mental fitness have a number of commonalities, the most important of which is the significance of paying attention to the routines you follow on a daily basis. These routines you do every day will pay off at crucial occasions when your mental fortitude is required as well.

Increasing one's mental toughness requires the cultivation of habits in each of the following 7 areas:

1. Mindfulness

Mindfulness training helps you become better at responding to situations rather than automatically reacting to them. It gives you the ability to slow down the stimulus-reaction loop, which enables you to choose a response that is effective for you. This ability will become useful in the long run, often when you are least expecting it yet could not get by without it. You could find that you are less inclined to get into arguments with your spouse or that you have less anxiety while speaking to your management.

There are many different ways to practice mindfulness, so choose one that appeals to you and is suitable for the way you live your life. Experiment with attentive breathing, try out walking meditation, or sign up for an online yoga session.

2. Enlist the assistance of a trained expert.

When it comes to building mental toughness, it may be quite beneficial to work with a mental health expert or a coach. After all, the struggle you face the most of the time takes place within your own thoughts. Both life coaches and therapists are particularly talented at teaching clients how to fight negative thinking patterns and break free from the unconscious control that these patterns exert over their actions.

Psychotherapists often accomplish this goal by engaging in cognitive behavioral therapy, also known as CBT. This method is particularly useful for the treatment of mental health conditions such as anxiety and depression. On the other side, coaches are able to assist give responsibility as their clients work towards achieving their objectives.

They have the ability to help you reframe negative experiences, preventing you from falling back into negative patterns, and keep you motivated.

3. Keep a diary or a journal.

Keeping a diary is an excellent option if you want to monitor your mental health on a consistent basis and keep track of your thoughts and feelings. It is an excellent tool for enhancing one's sense of self-worth since it enables one to monitor their own development over time and provide feedback on that development.

There are no restrictions on the kinds of things you may write in your journal. You may try freewriting for a few minutes, defining some goals for yourself, or making a list of the things that are causing you stress that feel especially overwhelming. Writing things down might sometimes assist our minds in beginning the process of working through difficulties that we are facing. It's a baby step toward getting over being overwhelmed and more towards feeling like you've got everything under control.

4. Have compassion for yourself and practice it.

Many of us have the misconception that berating ourselves would make us more productive in some way, but in reality, this could not be farther from the truth. The development of self-compassion is really beneficial to the development of resilience. A growth attitude may be maintained while avoiding a negative cycle if we avoid dwelling on our shortcomings and instead concentrate on what it is that we accomplish well. It makes it easier for us to say things like, "That didn't go so well, but here's what I learned — and how I can do better the next time."

5. Force yourself to step outside of your safe zone.

Do you want to find out whether you've acquired the fundamental abilities necessary for mental toughness? Put yourself in the middle of the action! Mental toughness is one of those qualities that, like many others, cannot be learned without consistent practice. It's a good thing that, at some time, you could be forced to engage in an activity that's novel, strange, or even a little bit terrifying.

Start small or start large – it doesn't matter. Register for a course, go out for a cup of coffee with someone who scares you, or submit an application for the job of your dreams on LinkedIn. Whatever it is, pay attention to how you react whenever you sense anxious sensations creeping up on you. Make a note of them in your notebook, and then reply to them as you would to a trusted friend. You will discover that you are capable of doing challenging tasks, and you may even find that you love them.

6. Establish a regular schedule for yourself.

You would be doing repetitions in the gym if you were trying to build up your physical strength. To increase your mental toughness, you should establish regular routines that serve to reinforce the newly acquired abilities that you are working on.

Keeping a journal, developing a mindfulness practice, and maintaining contact with a coach are all possible components of this regimen. You should give utmost importance to everything that prompts you to pause, contemplate, or ask questions. Make a conscious effort to think and act in ways that boost your self-assurance.

Make it a point to include activities that promote self-care into your day-to-day routine. People who are on the "personal development bandwagon" often have the perception that every aspect of their lives has to be "optimized" in order for them to be successful. Begin on a low scale and work your way up. Make fundamental aspects of your health a top priority, such as obtaining adequate rest, keeping an eye out for indicators of physical and mental exhaustion, and paying attention to what you put in your mouth.

7. Ensure that your relationships remain solid.

Relationships with other people are one of the factors that might tell us the most about how happy we will be in life. Do not attempt to do everything by yourself. We need to have loved ones around in order to enjoy our victories, be pushed to go on, and be comforted when things are difficult.

Your friends and family, as well as professionals such as a therapist or a coach, make up a significant part of your support system. Remember to take some time to relax and have fun. Have a good time, be with the people you care about, and engage in activities that provide joy to your life. Joy protects us from the negative effects of stress and energizes us to keep going even when we just want to give up.

To have strong mental fortitude is not the same as always pressing on, just as having strong physical fortitude does not need constant exercise. It's about being able to work and play, to love and lose, to push and praise, with equal ease and grace. Finding balance is about understanding how to do all of those things.

Chapter Twenty Four

Accepting what you can't control, taking responsibility for your actions, and concentrating on the lessons learned may be required in order to let go of the past, especially the individuals who have harmed you. Seeking assistance is another essential step.

The majority of individuals, at some time in their lives, have pondered the question of how to move on from a painful previous experience. It is only normal for you to have the feeling that the source of the emotional agony you are experiencing right now lies in the past. However, even if it was something that happened in the past, the first step in overcoming the pain is to concentrate on the present.

The question of how to move on from the past is likely to be interpreted differently by each individual. It might also depend on the circumstances of the case.

You could believe that letting go means being able to recall painful situations or individuals without feeling the associated emotional anguish. It's possible that you feel like it's about forgetting everything. Alternately, it might suggest that you wish to move on even if you haven't forgotten or forgiven the person yet.

It is possible to let go of whatever is weighing heavily on both your heart and head, whatever that may mean to you. You can heal, and the following advice may be of use to you.

Self Examination

When you've been injured for a long enough period of time, it's possible that you'll become accustomed to the emotional anguish. Perhaps you have a sense of comfort and recognition. It's possible that you've come to accept it as a fundamental aspect of who you are. Keeping your anger at that individual may make you feel more secure since it allows you to maintain your distance from them.

The discomfort of maturing may be quite genuine. It's possible that walking away from the things you've been thinking and feeling for a very long time can make you feel uneasy. On the other hand, it's possible that letting go may lead to healing, pleasure, and mental tranquility.

If you find yourself asking, "Why can't I let go?" then you could be one of the few people for whom this is true. These questions may assist you in beginning the process of letting go of the past:

Do you stand to gain anything additional if you continue to concentrate on the things that are causing you pain?

Does dwelling on the past prevent you from engaging in new relationships or experiencing new situations?

Do you avoid confronting the source of your emotional anguish since doing so would require you to resolve it?

What would your life be like if you stopped dwelling on the past and just moved on?

If you took on a different position in the circumstance, what do you think would happen?

Take In To Consideration:

Sometimes, in order to heal, you need to first allow yourself to experience it. It may be more detrimental to you in the long term and make it difficult to let go if you bottle up your thoughts and feelings. This is especially true if you keep thinking about the past and the things that have wronged you.

Your mood, your relationships, and even your capacity to be productive and creative might be negatively impacted if you keep thinking the same negative ideas over and over again.

You should make an effort to discover healthy methods to communicate how you are feeling. Getting rid of the emotional energy might make it easier for you to cease ruminating.

Think about participating in activities that will allow you to vent your emotions in a protected environment.

Accept Responsibility

When you take responsibility for your actions, it does not imply that you have to accept blame for things that have occurred to you in the past. Realizing how much of your energy you are devoting to remembering or experiencing things that are no longer part of your present is the first step in this process. It also involves making the conscious decision to direct your attention elsewhere.

When you refuse to let go of your sorrow, anger, or painful memories, you are forcing yourself to relive an unpleasant event over and over again. This may cause you to remain mired in the past, which is something that has passed and cannot be altered.

Accepting responsibility means you are also claiming your power and making the decision that you will not allow others to influence how you feel or how you conduct your life.

It's possible that you didn't have a choice in the matters that caused you pain in the past, but you have today. You have a choice today about where you will place your thoughts and feelings.

The perception that this is a challenging undertaking is normal and appropriate to have. Either the pain is so excruciating that you can't help but concentrate on it, or you have no choice but to deal with the repercussions of your actions. However, there is still hope for recovery.

If you're having trouble letting go of the past, you may want to talk to a mental health expert about how you can improve your coping skills and make it easier for yourself to move on. You deserve it.

Make An Effort

When you fixate on things that have happened in the past, you may not have much space in your heart and head for new experiences, especially ones that could offer you pleasure.

Your inability to let go of the past may increase the likelihood that you will overlook the positive aspects of your present.

Take into consideration the following actions to clear the way for the new and to let go of the old:

Establish personal as well as professional objectives for the near future.

Practice thankfulness in order to free your mind to concentrate on the excellent things happening right now.

Evaluate the quality of the connections you currently have and prioritize cultivating the ones that are beneficial to you.

Make it a monthly goal to try out a new pastime or activity, clean and arrange your areas so that you can donate or get rid of things that are no longer useful, and either form new connections or work on strengthening existing ones with people you already know but who have the potential to become lifelong companions.

Learn how to bring your attention back to the present moment whenever your thoughts stray to the future or the past by engaging in one act of self-care per week and practicing mindfulness.

Participate in charitable endeavors that might potentially improve your mood by assisting other people in finding good leaders and role models that are kind and empathic in their leadership.

Make You A Priority

Putting yourself first requires you to make deliberate choices in all aspects of your life. This might begin with the realization that selecting what is beneficial for oneself does not equate to acting in a self-centered manner.

Putting yourself first may also mean regaining your power by concentrating on healing in the here and now rather than dwelling on what has caused you pain in the past. It's about coming to terms with the fact that you do matter.

Consider:

Going to therapy to explore how to let go of the past and the hurt you've experienced, setting boundaries with other people who may want to relive or discuss the past when you're not ready to make life decisions that make you feel safe, at peace, or happy, even if others don't agree making life decisions that make you feel safe, at peace, or happy, making life decisions that make you feel safe, at peace, or happy, making life decisions that make you feel safe, at peace, or happy making life decisions

Putting yourself first could also mean looking into other avenues where you might find forgiveness.

It has been shown to be connected with improved levels of psychological well-being, such as a stronger tolerance for ambiguity and a lesser inclination to feel rage. This applies to forgiving both oneself and others.

Consider:

What have you discovered about life, yourself, relationships, and love as a result of the painful experiences you've had in the past?

Your first reaction to this inquiry could be to consider the unfavorable things you've picked up along the way. It makes sense and has merit. But make an effort to stop if this is your first response, and think about how you may instead concentrate on a few valuable lessons. Take, for instance:

What you now know you don't want in your life, how strong and resilient you may be, who stood by your side and showed you they are someone you can rely on, the coping skills you may have gained to deal with the difficulties that life throws at you, and how strong and resilient you may be.

The awareness that everything changes and that this, too, will eventually change

This is not a comprehensive list, and some of the items on it may not even be relevant to your circumstances.

The goal here is to examine how a traumatic experience
may have shaped you in positive ways, such as by
providing you with new abilities, insights, or information.
Keeping these lessons in mind may make it simpler to let
go of the past.

Acceptance

You can be dwelling on the events of the past because
you feel the need to reconsider the decisions you made in
the past or what might have been different.

If you are preoccupied with "what if" scenarios, you may
find that your thoughts keep returning to the same
conversations and situations. However, ruminating on
what took place won't make a difference in the outcome.

Learning to recognize the circumstances over which you
have no influence might be a step toward overcoming the
difficulties associated with letting go of the past.

The "should haves" or "what ifs" won't affect what really took place. The "what coulds" and "what wills" may be of assistance to you as you go ahead and attempt to be more purposeful in the choices that you make on a daily basis. These decisions will have an effect on both your present and your future.

Chapter Twenty Five

What Is Forgiveness?

The concept of "forgive and forget" is deeply ingrained in our society. This is the belief that in order to really forgive, we must first be able to forget the wrongs that have been committed against us.

This is utter nonsensicality.

It is quite improbable that you will ever be able to forget a significant wrong that has been perpetrated against you, unless you suffer from some type of serious neurological disorder.

However, if your standard for obtaining forgiveness is the deletion of the memory of the offense, you are setting yourself up for chronic dissatisfaction and even guilt since this is just not feasible on either a biological or a psychological level.

We may not be able to choose which memories remain in our minds, but we do have some say over how we focus our attention. To be more specific, we have the ability to exercise control over the extent to which we choose to concentrate on and brood over previous wrongs perpetrated against us.

Taking some time to think about what happened and work through your feelings about it is probably beneficial. It is a fallacy, however, to believe that you should let your attention to remain fixed on a particular idea or memory just because your mind is pulled to that concept or memory.

You will increase the likelihood that similar thoughts and memories may surface in the future if you choose to interact with and expand on these spontaneous recollections of your offender or the crime. If you choose to engage with and elaborate on these spontaneous memories of your offender or the offense. On the other hand, if you recognize them but then choose to re-focus your attention elsewhere, you will make it less likely that these memories will intrude on you in the future. This will make it easier for you to go on with your life.

Establish and stick to appropriate mental limits. Your state of mind will be grateful to you for it.

You can't control your memories, but you can control your attention.

Anger Vs. Forgiveness

It is natural for you to feel resentment against the person who wronged you. There are compelling evolutionary explanations for this, most of which have to do with the maintenance of social order and justice. It's true that anger may provide you a momentary rush of positive emotions and a boost to your ego.

But in the long term, unbridled anger tends to lead to unhealthy levels of mental elaboration over the wrongs done to you, which keeps those memories powerful and easily available in your memory. In other words, it keeps you angry for longer.

The less you mentally dwell on your resentment and the events that led up to it, the less often your mind will bring it up as a source of distraction for you.

When you become aware that you are feeling furious, give yourself a little pause and recognize that anger. At the same time, remind yourself that you have every right to be angry. But before you do that, you should ask yourself: Will it do me any good in the long run to continue to expand on what occurred and prolong my anger?

Even when you have good reason to be angry, it does not imply that acting on it will be productive. Your wrath is warranted, but you shouldn't add fuel to the fire.

Forgiveness Is Letting Go

Many individuals who have difficulty forgiving others have been offered the piece of advise that they should "accept" what has occurred and then go on with their lives. The issue is that words like "acceptance" are vague and may have several interpretations depending on who you ask.

When many people hear the word "accept," they automatically believe that it means endorsement, that you are somehow comfortable with what occurred or defending it. This is not the case.

But acceptance does not entail endorsement or justification. Many individuals who are already victims of an injustice are victimized more when they are led to believe that they were in some way responsible for the awful event that occurred to them by being tricked into believing this falsehood. That is hardly an example of acceptance.

Acknowledging that you do not have power or control over the past is an essential step toward acceptance.

It is very difficult for individuals who have been mistreated or otherwise harmed in some way to be able to accomplish this since it is human nature to feel more powerful when we believe we have some degree of control over the past.

However, in the end, it's all an illusion. The decision to let go of the need or desire to control the past is a necessary step in regaining command of one's future.

You don't have to make excuses for someone who wronged you in order to accept their apology.

Forgiveness Is Moving On

Many individuals who have been treated unfairly believe that they are obligated to try to make amends with the one who treated them unfairly.

People that come from very religious families seem to be more susceptible to this, in my experience. In spite of the fact that I am unable to comment on anybody else's particular religious views, I am aware of the fact that from a psychological point of view, reconciliation is not necessary in order to forgive. In point of fact, waiting for it to happen before forgiving someone might be counterproductive to the process of real forgiveness.

The difficulty that arises with forgiving someone on the condition that they make amends is that you cannot control the actions of other people. You are powerless to make the person who has harmed you realize the mistake of their ways, apologize from the bottom of their heart, and make amends so that the relationship may be repaired. This is true no matter how much you want it to happen. In addition, it is risky to use time and effort in the vain attempt to exert influence over factors that are ultimately beyond our control.

To be more specific, I've seen a lot of folks who are so intent — one would perhaps say obsessed — with making amends with their transgressor that they don't have enough mental and emotional energy left over to concentrate on the components of forgiveness over which they do have some level of influence. If I may put it another way, there is a significant potential cost associated with making forgiveness contingent upon reconciliation.

If you want to, you may hope for a reconciliation, but you shouldn't anticipate it.

Forgiveness May Take Time

One choice is all it takes to start the process of forgiving someone, but that's not where it stops.

Realize that forgiveness is a process and a journey rather than a single event, regardless of how many accounts you hear about the "moment of forgiveness."

The realization that this is just the beginning of the process of forgiving someone is a necessary and significant first step; nevertheless, it is crucial to keep in mind that this is only the beginning of the process. Along the path to forgiveness, there are likely to be a great number of further steps:

At subsequent family occasions, you will continue to run across the same relative with whom you had the argument.

Your traumatic experience will continue to resurface in your thoughts on occasion.

The efforts you make toward reconciliation will not be returned to you in kind.

It takes more than just one choice to forgive. Be ready to extend your forgiveness on a daily, weekly, and monthly basis. And even while it could grow simpler with the passage of time, forgiveness is something that lasts a lifetime.

It is not a choice to forgive someone; rather, it is an attitude and a mental habit.

Forgiveness Is A Decision

Many individuals have difficulty forgiving others because they mix the act of forgiving with the emotional response they anticipate feeling as a result of forgiving. To be more specific, the majority of individuals who have difficulty forgiving someone badly want to feel better. They want to have mental peace, less wrath and hatred, quiet and equanimity, and maybe even compassion or love for their offender or the person who is responsible for their harm. Forgiveness may be a difficult process for many people.

However, how we feel as a result of forgiving others is not forgiveness itself; rather, it is a byproduct of forgiving. To add insult to injury, the emotions that may or may not surface as a result of exercising forgiveness are not always the same. They might seem quite different from one another based on the particular persons and situations that are in play.

There is no universally applicable rule that states, "If you forgive someone, you will definitely feel more at peace as a result of it." Realizing that how you feel emotionally in response to a significant wrong done to you is not fundamentally within your control is one of the things that makes real forgiveness one of the most difficult things to do. In point of fact, this is one of the factors that makes it so tough.

You are able to exercise control over your actions, such as how you think and how you behave, including the option to forgive, but the way we feel is not something that is directly within our control.

People certainly have a tendency to feel better as a consequence of forgiving others, but it is unwise to anticipate a particular range of emotions as a result of this act.

The ability to forgive is more of a decision than an emotion.

Forgive You

When we have been treated unfairly, our range of feelings is often dominated by one or two strong feelings, one of which is rage in its many forms. These feelings may be culturally ingrained. On the other hand, the path to forgiveness usually always involves the presence of other feelings, all of which should be taken into consideration.

Develop the practice of searching beyond and under the emotions that are most visible to you in order to recognize the subtler, more subdued ones. These feelings, for instance, are just as legitimate as your anger, but they have the potential to be more beneficial.

For instance, if you give yourself permission to experience feelings of melancholy, sorrow, and sympathy as a result of what took happened, you may be able to look at the offender and the act from a different perspective.

In turn, this may help you think differently about and behave in new ways, maybe in a manner that is more aligned with your long-term beliefs and your desire to forgive and let go of the past.

Embrace the uniqueness, from a psychological standpoint, of your own path to forgiveness.

Everything that you absolutely must be aware of.

All too often, when we consider forgiveness, we do it in nebulous ethical or philosophical terms. However, at its core, the process of forgiving an offense is psychological rather than moral:

What are the mental practices that really liberate us from the effects of our previous transgressions and wrongdoings?

What kinds of choices can we make and what kinds of activities can we devote ourselves to that will bring us genuine mental tranquility?

Which aspect of our connection to the past is most likely to facilitate our progress toward the future?

In order to discover true forgiveness and be able to go on with our life, we need to have an understanding of the psychology of forgiveness, which may at times seem counterintuitive, and we need to be committed to making our own individual journey toward genuine peace and freedom.